Boys and Literacy

- What are boys' apparent difficulties with literacy?
- How are these difficulties related to gender?
- Can schools actually improve boys' attainment in literacy?

The phenomenon of the under-achieving boy is a major concern to governments across the Western world. Reports of a growing anti-school culture and the direct link that is said to exist between boys' under-achievement, truancy and crime have fuelled anxieties about boys' attainment in school. It is against this background of moral panic that the staff of a primary school in South Wales decided to explore the 'boys and literacy' issue for themselves. This book tells the story of that school's exploration.

Boys and Literacy: Exploring the issues provides a detailed look at the perceptions and practice of teachers in one school and the changes that occurred as these teachers struggled to make sense of the complex relationship that exists between gender, school and literacy. The study has fascinating implications for all those involved in education, gender, literacy and school improvement, and will be of particular interest to undergraduate and masters levels students.

Trisha Maynard is a Senior Lecturer in the Department of Education, University of Wales Swansea.

Language and Literacy in Action Series
Series Editor: David Wray

Teaching Literacy Effectively in the Primary School
David Wray and Jane Medwell

Boys and Literacy: Exploring the Issues
Trisha Maynard

Raising Standards in Literacy
Edited by Ros Fisher, Maureen Lewis and Greg Brooks

Boys and Literacy
Exploring the issues

Trisha Maynard

London and New York

First published 2002 by RoutledgeFalmer
11 New Fetter Lane, London EC4P 4EE

Simultaneously published in the USA and Canada
by RoutledgeFalmer
29 West 35th Street, New York, NY 10001

RoutledgeFalmer is an imprint of the Taylor & Francis Group

© 2002 Trisha Maynard

Typeset in Sabon by Taylor & Francis Books Ltd
Printed and bound in Great Britain by TJ International Ltd,
Padstow, Cornwall

British Library Cataloguing in Publication Data
A catalogue record for this book is available from the British Library.

Library of Congress Cataloging in Publication Data
Maynard, Trisha. Boys and literacy : exploring the issues /
Trisha Maynard. (Language and literacy in action)
Includes bibliographical references and index
1. Boys–Education–Great Britain. 2. Language arts–Social
aspects–Great Britain. 3. Underachievers–Great Britain.
4. Academic achievement–Great Britain. 5. Sex differences in
education–Great Britain. I. Title. II. Series
LC1390 .M39 2001
371.93 212001048167

ISBN 0–415–23760–2 (hbk)
ISBN 0–415–23761–0 (pbk)

This book is written in memory of my past – my parents, Rose Eveleen Alton (1917–1999) and John Leonard Alton (1919–2000); in celebration of my present – in particular, my husband David; and with hope for my future – our children Rosie and Jack.

Contents

Series editor's preface

David Wray, University of Warwick

There can be few areas of educational endeavour which have been more controversial than that of teaching literacy. Perhaps because, in an increasingly information-dense society, the ability to make sense of and to produce text is self-evidently crucial to success, even survival, literacy has assumed the major burden as a litmus test of 'educatedness'. With such a critical role in the process of becoming educated, it is inevitable that there will continue to be major debates about exactly what it means to be literate, and about how such a state might most effectively be brought about – that is, how literacy is taught. A proportion of the energy behind such debates has come from the diverse findings of research into processes and pedagogy. Yet much of the debate, especially in the popular media, has lacked a close reference to research findings and has focused instead on somewhat emotional reactions and prejudices.

Students of literacy and literacy education who want to move beyond the superficiality of mass media debates need access to reports and discussions of key research findings. There is plenty of such material, yet it tends to suffer from two major problems. First, it can be rather difficult to locate as it has tended to be published in a diverse range of academic journals, papers and monographs. Second, research reports are usually written for an academic audience and made great demands on practitioners and others who wish to understand what the practical classroom implications are of what the research reports.

It is to address both these problems, but especially the latter, that this series has been developed. The books in the series deal with aspects of the teaching of literacy and language in a variety of educational settings. The main feature of all the contributing volumes is to provide a research-grounded background for teaching action in literacy and language. The books either, therefore, provide a review of existing research and theory, or an account of original research in an area, together with a clear résumé and/or set of suggestions as to how this background might influence the teaching of this area. The series acts therefore as a bridge between academic research books and practical teaching handbooks.

Boys and Literacy

In this volume Tricia Maynard tackles an issue which has been widely discussed in recent years and whose ramifications have troubled everyone from politicians downwards. As yearly SATs results continue to suggest, the under-achievement of boys has become one of those seemingly endemic educational problems to which there are, apparently, no straightforward solutions. Just what is it about boys, and boy culture, which leads to under-achievement in this, the most vital aspect of learning?

Tricia approaches this problem not through a wide-ranging statistically based attempt to identify causal factors, nor, indeed, in search of the 'magic bullet' which might put things right. Instead she presents an in-depth study of a school and a group of teachers who set out to explore the issue within their own, local context. This exploration leads to some fascinating reflections on the nature of the difficulties boys appear to have with literacy, the contexts and learning experiences which appear to either cause problems or allow boys to shine, and the teachers' own prejudices about the capabilities of their male pupils. In particular, the ubiquitous practice of story writing is examined and questioned.

This is a brave book in that it presents an honest account of a group of teachers desperate to do their best for their pupils, but groping towards an understanding of just what that might look like. Teachers wishing to undertake this thoughtful process for themselves will find it a readable and stimulating account.

Acknowledgements

First and foremost I want to thank Dave and all the teachers and children at St Thomas Primary School – I feel privileged to have worked with you all! In addition, I wish to express my gratitude to Gill Harper-Jones, Kathy Lowe and Phil Jackson for their support in the early stages of this research. Thanks also to Tracey Kent for covering for my frequent absences from the department while I struggled to complete this book and to Madeleine Rogerson and the staff in the Education Library for their patience and efficiency. Finally, my thanks go to those friends and colleagues who learnt not to ask, 'Is it finished yet?'

Introduction

In the last decade of the twentieth century, across the Western world, the phenomenon of the 'poor', 'lost' and 'under-achieving' boy came into the media spotlight. It is the idea that boys are '*under*-achieving' that is of particular significance to this book. What is meant by this term? Does it, perhaps, reflect a belief that boys are not fulfilling their innate potential or reaching expected levels of attainment? Or does it reflect a fundamental concern about boys' attainment relative to the attainment of girls? And how did this concern with boys' under-achievement come about?

In the 1980s it was *girls'* poor attainment in the 'harder-edged', traditionally male subjects such as mathematics and science that was considered problematic. By the 1990s, however, this was to change. National tests and examination results revealed that girls were catching up with and in some cases overtaking boys in these subject areas. At the same time, in the 'soft' subjects in which girls had traditionally excelled, boys were found to be still trailing behind. This was particularly the case in English, where concerns about boys' attainment in reading and, in particular, in writing, became the focus of a great deal of research, government report-writing and media speculation.

It is likely that concerns about boys' attainment in literacy at this time were amplified by fears of a hardening anti-school and anti-learning culture amongst boys, a supposed 'direct' link between under-achievement, truancy and crime and a much-publicised crisis of masculinity itself. Certainly, by the mid-1990s the problem of the under-achieving boy was described as 'one of the biggest challenges facing society today' (Wragg, 1997).

It is against such a backdrop of media, governmental and moral panic, that teachers at a primary school in South Wales decided to explore the 'boys and literacy' issue for themselves. This book tells the story of that one school's explorations. I do not attempt, then, to present a broad, statistical analysis of the nature of the 'problem'. Nor do I try to identify a 'solution', nor suggest a list of potential strategies that might be used as a 'remedy' for this problem. Rather, this book provides a small, detailed, close-up look at ordinary (extraordinary) teachers struggling to make sense of the complexities of gender and its impact on literacy and to do their best to improve the learning and life-chances of their pupils. The aim of this book therefore, above all, is to encourage and support other schools in engaging in their own explorations of this and other issues.

The setting

My own interest in this project dates back to the late 1990s when Dave, the head teacher, contacted me to ask whether I would be willing to become involved in a whole-school investigation of boys' difficulties with literacy. He explained that, for many years, the teachers at St Thomas Primary School[1] had recognised that more boys than girls were having problems with speaking, reading and, in particular, with writing. This awareness had already sparked a number of initiatives within the school. For example, in order to motivate the poorer readers – who were mainly boys – pupils had visited a local bookshop to choose books for the school library. Before they were put on display, each book was stamped with the name of the child who had chosen it; this was to be seen as a personal recommendation. However, Dave was concerned that such initiatives may only be 'chipping away' at the surface of the problem. He wanted to make the 'boys and literacy' issue a focus of school improvement for all members of staff.

Dave also expressed his concern that there were a number of problems within the school that potentially could 'dent' staff morale. Standing as a landmark on the side of Kilvey Hill, overlooking Swansea City and the docks, the imposing Victorian red brick building had slipped into a state of disrepair and decay. A new school has now been promised but at the time of this project no such offer was forthcoming and teachers and pupils had to contend with rain regularly leaking into several of the classrooms and on to the spiral stone staircases linking the three floors. As well as problems with the fabric of the building, Dave was also concerned that every year there appeared to be increasing numbers of children with social and learning difficulties moving into the area: this inevitably impacted on the school's Standard Assessment Tasks (SATs) results. Dave maintained that exploring the 'boys and literacy' issue as a whole-school project, while being valuable in its own right, would also have the advantage of 'pulling the staff together' in the face of such challenges.

The school and its staff were known to me: as a lecturer on the Primary Postgraduate Certificate of Education (PGCE) I had in the past been the link tutor at this school and (hopefully) had established positive working relationships with many of the teachers. However, I was initially uncertain about accepting Dave's invitation. While I was eager to support my teacher colleagues, the project had no external funding and therefore I had no way of buying myself out of any of my existing work commitments. Moreover, while I was interested in the 'boys and literacy' issue, it was not an area in which I had any particular experience or expertise. Having voiced these concerns to Dave, within a few days he telephoned to assure me that the Local Education Authority (LEA) English Adviser had agreed to take a particular interest in this project and that, essentially, my role would be to help structure and support the school-based research. Despite my initial concerns, then, the prospect of becoming involved in a collaborative, whole-school project and the enthusiasm demonstrated by Dave and the teachers became irresistible. Who, then, were the teachers with whom I would work? What were their current classes and (shared) areas of curriculum responsibility?

The main characters

At the time of this project, Jacqui (Reception) had been at St Thomas for the eight years since she qualified as a teacher and was responsible for Art and Design and English. Melanie (Reception/Year 1) had been a teacher for twelve years; St Thomas was the second school at which she had taught. Her curriculum responsibilities were for history, mathematics and information and communication technology (ICT). Gaynor (Year 1) had over twenty years' teaching experience and had taught in several schools before joining the staff at St Thomas. Gaynor's curriculum responsibilities were for Welsh and design and technology (DT). Emma (Year 2) and Paula (Year 2/3) came to St Thomas as newly qualified teachers and had been teaching for five years. Emma was responsible for geography, physical education (PE) and music, Paula for English and science.

Glenda (Year 4), the deputy head teacher, had been qualified for sixteen years and had been a member of staff at St Thomas for fourteen years. She was responsible for ICT, DT, and art and design. Simon (Year 5) had been a teacher for twelve years and had taught in three schools before coming to St Thomas. His areas of responsibility were PE and history. Like Simon, Amanda (Year 5/6) joined the staff five years ago, but as a newly qualified teacher. Her current areas of responsibility were science and Welsh. Christine (Year 6) had only been at St Thomas for two years, although in the twelve years since she qualified she had taught in both primary and secondary schools as well as in Higher Education. Christine was responsible for music and mathematics. Gareth had been a member of staff of St Thomas for ten years and had over twenty years' teaching experience. Gareth was responsible for teaching the children with special educational needs and so did not have a designated class. He also took responsibility for the teaching of religious education within the school. Finally, Dave had taught for twenty-three years and had been the head teacher of St Thomas for eight years. In addition to his role as head teacher, Dave took responsibility for the teaching of English and geography.

The project

The project ran for approximately eighteen months. I worked with two university colleagues who had a particular interest in language and literacy (Gill Harper-Jones and Kathy Lowe). Gill, Kathy and I met the staff to discuss their initial ideas and concerns as well and to explain some of the key principles and processes of school-based (action) research; at this meeting I suggested that it might be useful to begin the research by exploring teachers' perceptions about boys' and literacy. With the support of Kathy Lowe, therefore, each of the teachers was interviewed individually.

Having examined teachers' *perceptions* of boys' difficulties there was then a recognised need to explore their *actual* difficulties. A sample group of six children in each class was identified and all writing undertaken by these children was collected by their teachers over a six-week period. This writing was analysed in different ways by the head teacher, the teachers and by myself. Later that year I also interviewed the 'sample' children in order to establish their ideas about the teaching and learning of literacy.

In one sense, these early phases of the research were seen as a way of collecting baseline evidence for the teachers' own research projects. The teachers set about devising and piloting a number of strategies that aimed to improve the teaching and learning of literacy in their school. Christmas intervened and this work was 'put on hold' until the following January. In May, I interviewed teachers about their progress and in July I conducted the final interviews to find out what teachers felt they had learnt through involvement in the project.

The main themes

What was discovered about boys' difficulties with literacy, then, forms a central theme of this book. I chart teachers' initial perceptions of these difficulties and how their perceptions changed over time. During the course of the project it became apparent that boys' difficulties were, in general, less obvious than teachers had thought initially. Moreover, I suggest that difficulties relating to transcription (spelling, handwriting and punctuation), which are common to many poor writers, may have become 'owned' by boys – that is, they have become seen as 'gendered'. At the end of the project it was noted that the only area of gender difference uncontested by teachers related to attitudes, interests and behaviour and how these impacted on children's preferences and attainment in writing.

A second theme of this book is that of change – particularly in relation to teachers' practice. Teachers maintained that, as the project progressed, their practice became more focused and structured, and they made greater use of direct teaching. In addition, the significance of story writing and its importance in the primary school was questioned as they shifted their emphasis on to teaching other forms of writing. I discuss those factors teachers felt were significant in supporting change, although I note that it would be wrong to claim that change took place as a direct result of involvement in this research; these changes closely reflect the 'spirit of the age'.

As well as looking at the detail of teachers' practice, I also attempt to ground this exploration within a broader, political and historical context. Here I touch on changes in attitudes towards women and the world of work during the last century and note that while it is claimed the work-place has now become more feminised, at the same time attempts are being made to masculinise schooling. Why is this happening? And why have concerns about educational attainment become almost solely defined in relation to gender rather than, for example, socio-economic background or race? Is it that, given government concerns about competing in a global market, there is a realisation that literacy matters and that, in relation to literacy, gender is seen as the most powerful divider? Or is it that presenting the problem as one of gender ensures that this particular story has a victim (males), a culprit (females), a crime (the feminisation of schooling) and a solution (more male teachers and role-models and the adoption of boy-friendly teaching methods)?

In conclusion, I suggest that, while the teachers in this study recognised that the relationship between gender, literacy and boys' under-achievement was complex, they felt that it was not within their role to consider issues or contributory factors that were 'outside the school gates'. Rather, within the constraints of the need to use 'legitimate' literature, they saw their job as one of raising standards of attainment as they are defined by policy-makers and assessed by Standard Assessment Tasks (SATs). The third theme of this book, then, is one of power, patriarchy, autonomy and resistance.

A brief outline of the book

The book is organised in three parts, drawing (broadly) on the main elements of story structure: 'Setting the scene', 'Complications' and 'Towards a resolution?' Chapter 1 begins by sketching in the historical and political context. In Chapter 2 there is a consideration of the various theories that have been proposed to explain gender differences and how these might relate to children's preferences and attainment in literacy. Chapter 3 briefly comments on the School Effectiveness and School Improvement movements before going on to consider the broad framework of school-based action research and discussing a number of relevant research methods and issues.

Part II of the book incorporates Chapters 4 to 7, which document the various phases of the project and demonstrate how, as the research progressed, the 'boys and literacy' issue came to be seen in more complex ways. Chapter 4 describes what was found to be the teachers' perceptions of boys' difficulties, Chapter 5 explores our attempts to analyse samples of children's writing, while Chapter 6 considers children's perceptions of literacy in school. The teachers' individual and collaborative research projects are reported and discussed in Chapter 7.

Part III of the book, 'Towards a resolution?' consists of the final chapter, Chapter 8, in which I draw together the main themes of this book based around my final interviews with the teachers at the end of the academic year.

Part I
Setting the scene

1 The context
A problem of gender

In 1996 Chris Woodhead, then Chief Inspector of Ofsted (Office for Standards in Education), was reported in *The Times Educational Supplement* (*TES*) as stating: 'the failure of boys and in particular white working-class boys is one of the most disturbing problems we face within the whole education system' (Pyke 1996). A year later Ted Wragg maintained that it is 'the under-achievement of boys that has become one of the biggest challenges facing society today (1997). Such headlines, while in one sense shocking, were – and continue to be – fairly commonplace. Indeed, from the early 1990s the problem of the 'under-achieving boy' has rarely been out of the media. Boys are frequently portrayed as loutish, lazy, 'lads' caught up in an anti-school, anti-learning culture. This culture, according to the then government's Education Secretary, David Blunkett, has grown out of 'deprivation and a lack of self-confidence and opportunity' (Woodward 2000).

Politicians – for example, Estelle Morris (1996) and Stephen Byers (cited in Lepkowska 1998) have emphasised the direct link that is believed to exist between under-achievement in school and truancy and crime. But it is not simply the cost of crime at a local level that is seen as a cause for concern but the damage that is being done to society as a whole. Thus concerns about the 'laddish' anti-learning culture have resulted in a 'moral panic' – that is, this culture is seen 'as a threat to societal values and interests' (Cohen 1987: 9). But how has this situation come about? Who is seen as to blame? And what are the suggested solutions? This is the focus of Chapter 1. In order to explore these questions I refer not only to writers of academic texts but also to the voices of politicians and others as reported in the media – this has, after all, been a drama played out on a public stage. First, however, I will sketch in the historical and political context; it is necessary to understand this context if we are to make sense of the current concerns about under-achieving boys.

The historical and political context

Measor and Sikes (1992) point to the long history of education and schooling being closely tied up with views of femininity and masculinity and the sexual division of labour. They maintain that even before the 1870 Education Act females were taught that males were superior to them in every way – physically, intellectually, morally and socially – and that as women their role in life was to serve and service men. What has come to be termed 'Victorian values' reinforced the view that men and women inhabited 'separate spheres': 'the public world of work and achievement was to be occupied by the independent and autonomous male and the private, enclosed domain of the "home, care, harmony and relationships" by the intuitive and dependent female' (Brabeck 1996, cited in Arnot *et al.* 1999: 34).

As Arnot *et al.* (1999) explain, this view is linked to what are seen as biologically derived 'natural' male and female characteristics (see Chapter 2). Thus, they argue, with the creation of a national system of education in the late nineteenth century, boys and girls were educated according to their gender[1] as well as their class. Upper- and middle-class males were essentially prepared for leadership roles whereas working-class boys were schooled for the manual labour force. Similarly, upper- and middle-class girls were taught household management whereas working-class females learned housework and laundry skills. Girls' education (whatever their class) was linked to what was seen as girls' eventual destiny as wives and mothers (Arnot *et al.* 1999). This was supported by a proposed connection between female over-education – that is, mental strain – and infertility (Measor and Sikes 1992). As Measor and Sikes (1992) point out, middle-class girls who *were* educated usually had to make a choice between a career on the one hand or marriage and motherhood on the other.

Post-war education

In the first half of the twentieth century, challenges to Victorian values were mounted from the women's movement, those advocating social democracy and the 1944 Education Act which, in theory at least, supported equality of opportunity (Arnot *et al.* 1999). Measor and Sikes (1992) note that, despite these challenges, various reports (e.g. the *Hadow Report* 1926; the *Crowther Report* 1959; the *Newsom Report* 1963) appeared to accept the 'common-sense' view that boys and girls should be prepared for the different roles they were to fulfil in adult life. As Arnot *et al.* (1999) explain, while there was now the expectation that boys and girls should have equal 'access' to education, there was not the expectation that this equality would follow on into the world of work.

Outside the school walls

Outside the school walls, in the early years of the twentieth century, women's dependency on men was reinforced by their low rates of pay – this applied even to jobs taken up by middle-class women such as teaching, nursing and clerical work (Rowbotham 1999). With the outbreak of the First World War, however, the notion of a segregated jobs market was set aside as women were recruited to work in industry. Rowbotham (1999) notes that even protective legislation was waived so that women could work at night – thus enabling them to do their housework during the day!

As war ended, however, there was strong pressure on these women to relinquish their jobs in order to make way for the men and, during the 1920s and 1930s, the idea of woman as homemaker and full-time mother was promoted. However, as Rowbotham (1999) explains, the declaration of war in 1939 created a problem for the government: how could this ideal be safeguarded when women were needed yet again to make up the short-fall in the workforce? The solution, Rowbotham notes, was the introduction of National Service for single, childless women aged 20–30. In addition, fears that some women might be deterred by the idea of working long hours led to the introduction of the possibility of part-time work.

Following the war, Beveridge's vision of the welfare state was intended – yet again – to promote the idea of the man as breadwinner and head of the household with the woman playing a supportive role as full-time wife and mother. However, as Arnot *et al.* (1999) point out, an unintended consequence of the welfare state was the expansion of employment opportunities for women within the welfare and service industries. But just as more married mothers began to go out to work in the 1950s, new ideas about child-rearing practices revived concerns about women's role. Prominent amongst these were the theories of John Bowlby who stressed the importance of the young child's need for a continuous relationship with the mother: indeed, any separation from the mother was viewed as 'deprivation' and as potentially damaging.

Even so, in the 1960s and first half of the 1970s the number of women in paid work increased, although the notion of separate labour markets for men and women persisted and women continued to earn a great deal less than men. However, attitudes had begun to change, influenced, in part, by the Civil Rights and Women's Liberation movements in the USA (Weiner 1985). Women demanded equal educational opportunities for boys and girls and child-care for pre-school children. Arnot *et al.* (1999) note that the one official policy which attempted to accommodate some of these ideas was the Sex Discrimination Act of 1975.

The aim of the Sex Discrimination Act, according to Arnot *et al.* (1999), was to create a more gender-neutral educational framework. For example, it now became illegal to exclude pupils from taking particular school subjects on the grounds of their sex, although in practice boys and girls continued (and still continue) to make stereotypical subject choices. Most significantly, perhaps, the Act did open up spaces for feminists to campaign for equality of opportunity in schools, gather evidence on the unequal treatment of girls and to call for action (Gaine and George 1999).

But despite the growing interest in equal opportunities by parents, teachers and the government alike, it appeared that while supporting this development in theory, in practice many teachers argued that their role was to prepare pupils for 'society as it was' (Figes 1994).

Weiner (1985) maintains that government interest in the development of anti-sexist practices in school at this time had its origins in the sustained economic and educational growth of the 1960s and 1970s. If the country needed more skilled labour then (as during both world wars) the government was prepared to ensure legislation did not prevent women from meeting this need. Weiner notes that, although driven by different motives, it seemed at this point as if the interests of the legislators on the one hand and activist teachers and parents on the other were beginning to converge. However, by the late 1970s the period of post-war boom had ended and, as the country slid into recession and unemployment began to grow, the Conservative government of the day grew less interested in equity issues and again began to promote the ideals of motherhood and domesticity (Weiner 1985). Gradually, the discourse of equality gave way to New Right notions of 'individualism', 'competition' and 'performance' (Arnot *et al.* 1999). By the late 1980s, government interest had shifted away from gender differences in policy and practice and towards issues such as patterns of gender difference in examination results (Gipps and Murphy 1994).

'Women are doing it for themselves'

All the while, the predominantly female workforce of teachers had been sowing the seeds of change, supported by research findings which, as David *et al.* (2000) note, pointed to the shortcomings of schooling for girls. By the early 1980s, some teachers and LEAs began to develop strategies to address these inequalities (David *et al.* 2000). There was a particular concern to encourage girls to study what were seen as traditionally 'male' subjects such as science, mathematics and technology. Arnot *et al.* (1999) note that, in encouraging and supporting girls' involvement in the most consistently male-dominated subject areas, an emphasis was placed on the significance of female role models as well as addressing the learning styles favoured by girls and 'the masculine content and orientation of most textbooks, topics and tests' (Arnot *et al.* 1999: 78).

Weiner (1985) comments that two distinct approaches to challenging sex discrimination in school emerged at this time: the equal opportunities approach and the anti-sexist approach. The equal opportunities approach, associated with liberal feminism, concentrated on equality of access to existing educational benefits for both boys and girls. This included an improvement of teaching methods for the benefit of all pupils, devising non-sexist materials aimed at challenging gender stereotypes, de-sexing registers and school uniform and, as we have seen, persuading girls to take subjects such as science and technology (Weiner and Arnot 1987).

Anti-sexist approaches, on the other hand, took a more radical stance and aimed to make school more 'girl-centred'. This approach was more concerned with equality of outcome and recognised the need to 'redress past imbalances' (Riley 1994: 13). Weiner (1985) notes that central to this approach was a recognition of the relationship between patriarchy, power and women's subordination. Those advocating this approach wanted a fundamental restructuring of the whole school system and to overthrow the male domination of curricula, classrooms and schools (Weiner 1994).

Unsurprisingly, perhaps, it was the liberal feminist 'equal opportunities' approach that was (and still is) most favoured by the government and local education authorities. And, it could be argued, it was this approach that was also reflected in the introduction of the National Curriculum and Statutory Assessment requirements in July 1988. Based on the concept of entitlement, the National Curriculum set out a common set of subjects to be taken by girls and boys up to the age of 16 some of which were to be assessed through Standard Assessment Tasks (SATs). And it was with the introduction of the National Curriculum that the pattern of subject choices that had been shaped by Victorian values appeared to be finally broken (Arnot *et al.* 1999).

The National Curriculum has not been without its critics. Gaine and George (1999), for example, comment that the rigid and fixed nature of this curriculum only serves to reinforce traditional values upheld by white, male-dominated areas of knowledge. Nor, they argue, does it challenge boys' and girls' subject choices, teachers' expectations or the pervasive 'informal' curriculum.

The 1990s

If during most of the twentieth century there had been concerns about girls' under-achievement in school, in the 1990s these concerns were reversed: it is boys who are now seen as having difficulties. Moreover, underlying these difficulties is a concern that boys' under-achievement is not only linked to truancy and crime but to a more fundamental crisis: that of masculinity itself. Estelle Morris (1996) has argued that this crisis has come about as, in the past, young men who did not achieve academically had the chance to take up apprenticeships and to be self-reliant within a framework of the traditional family unit. But, as we have seen, manual work – particularly in the manufacturing industries – is no longer a viable option for these boys. In addition, the 'traditional' family unit (with man as head of the household and main breadwinner) has become something of a rarity. As a result, Morris claims, many young men have become disaffected, marginalised from mainstream society and trapped within a culture of dependency.

But recent changes appear to have had a much more positive effect on young women. As we have seen, the growth of the service sector and information technology has resulted in more jobs for women – even if these tend to be temporary and low-paid. Moreover, changes in employment patterns have contributed towards what has been described as the feminisation of work (Stainton Rogers and Stainton Rogers 2001). Stainton Rogers and Stainton Rogers (2001) maintain that, in the new jobs market, men's traditional strengths, such as their physical prowess and competitiveness, are seen as a less valuable asset than women's traditional strengths – flexibility, adaptability and cooperation. Consequently, not only have women become more employable but pressure has been put on men to adopt what are viewed as more feminine traits.

As a result of these changes it is suggested that, compared with men, young women generally have greater self-esteem, are happier, more ambitious and more positive about the future (Stainton Rogers and Stainton Rogers 2001). Having broken out of their traditional sphere of home and dependency, women are redefining femininity and, as a consequence, requiring masculinity to be redefined. But definitions of masculinity, it is argued, appear resistant to change – Arnot *et al.* (1999) indicate that this may be because, unlike generations of women and girls, men are not used to being challenged to make personal, social, educational and occupational changes. While some men have been successful in making the necessary adjustments in terms of their masculine identity, others have failed to do so and have adopted a position of hyper-masculinity: the stereotypical macho man (Stainton Rogers and Stainton Rogers 2001).

As we shall see in Chapter 2, boys often construct and display their knowledge of masculinity through adopting a position of hegemonic[2] masculinity: through playing the fool, engaging in anti-social behaviour and adopting an anti-school, anti-learning stance. For some boys the lure of hegemonic masculinity may be limited in both time and intensity. For example, it may be offset by other factors, such as home circumstances which challenge such behaviour, convey high expectations, encourage self-belief and provide material and emotional support. Other boys may find its appeal overwhelming – positioning themselves as a 'macho man' offers them a means (possibly the only means) by which they can claim power and status in the world.

How, then, have these more fundamental difficulties with masculinity been reflected in the attainment of boys in school?

The gender gap

In this era of standards and performance, it is unsurprising that boys' difficulties have become visible through the published results of national tests and examinations. And, since the early 1990s, concerns have been raised not simply about boys' attainment but about the relative attainment of boys and girls – what has become known as the 'gender gap'. By the end of the 1990s it was noted, for example, that more girls than boys achieved five A*–C grades at GCSE. While results were similar in mathematics and science, girls did better than boys in subjects such as history, geography and Information Technology (IT) and, in particular, in English, modern languages, and art and design. More boys than girls were leaving school with no GCSE passes while the vast majority of pupils being permanently excluded from school (figures for 1997/8) were boys. In addition, two out of three pupils in special schools were boys (figures for 1998/9; from the DfEE Standards Site: www.standards.dfee.gov.uk).

At Key Stages 1 (KS1), 2 (KS2) and 3 (KS3) a similar pattern emerged. For example, the 1999 results in mathematics and science were broadly comparable, although in the English SAT around 10 per cent more girls than boys achieved the 'expected' levels of attainment in KS1 and KS2. Moreover, at KS2, while boys had made considerable improvements in reading to narrow the 'gender gap' to six percentage points, the gap between boys' and girls' writing stood at fifteen percentage points. By KS3 the gap between boys' and girls' results in English increased to eighteen percentage points. In Wales the statistics for 1999 followed a similar pattern to those in England with the gender gap only being striking in the results for Welsh and English (see www. education.wales.gov.uk).

In England, a concern with standards of attainment in English, as well as the use of particular teaching methods in schools, led to the introduction of the National Literacy Strategy (NLS). This strategy includes a framework for a daily hour of the explicit teaching of reading and writing, focusing on aspects of language such as phonics, spelling, grammar and punctuation. Based on the introduction of the NLS, David Blunkett, the then Secretary of State for Education and Employment, set a target of 80 per cent of 11-year-olds achieving the standards of literacy expected for their age by 2002 – that is level 4. (In Wales, this target is set at between 70 per cent and 80 per cent of 11-year-olds attaining level 4 or above in English and Welsh.) In order to help children reach these targets, since 2000 schools in England have received additional funding to be spent on 'booster' classes for children on the borderline between level 3 and 4 (Ofsted 2001).

Size matters?

It is, however, the size of the gender gap – the relative attainment of boys and girls in English – which appears to preoccupy researchers, the government and the media alike. In January 1999 it was reported that the gender gap had 'widened to a gulf' (Cassidy 1999). By October, following the analysis of another year's test results, it was announced that boys had 'turned the tide' in literacy (Thornton 1999), although a further report on the same day maintained that 'Boys Close Reading Gap but Still Trail in Writing' (Hackett 1999).

But these headlines only tell part of the story. A closer look at the 1999 (Key Stages 1 and 2) results for Wales, for example, indicate that in the English SAT at KS1 a higher percentage of boys than girls were working at below level 2 – the expected level of attainment – in both reading and writing. Moreover, when examining the 'fine-grading' of level 2 (that is, levels 2a, 2b and 2c), it is apparent that boys were achieving at the lower end of 'average' – particularly in writing. Overall, the figures indicate that the number of boys and girls achieving level 2 were comparable in reading with girls taking the lead in writing: 76 per cent of girls compared with 71 per cent of boys achieved level 2. However, the number of boys attaining level 3 (above the expected level of attainment) in reading was 20 per cent compared with 31 per cent of girls. In writing, this figure was 5 per cent of boys compared with 11 per cent of girls. Similarly, at KS2 the number of boys and girls achieving the 'required' level 4 in the English test/task appears not to be too dissimilar: 46 per cent for boys and 48 per cent for girls. However the number of boys achieving above level 4 was 17 per cent compared with 26 per cent of girls.

These results indicate that while the number of boys and girls achieving 'expected' levels of attainment in English were, in fact, broadly comparable (or at least the difference between them was less extreme) a higher percentage of boys than girls were represented in the lower levels of attainment. In addition, a higher percentage of girls than boys were represented in the higher levels of attainment. If there is or ever was a 'gulf' between boys' and girls' results, it appears to be related essentially to children performing at the extremes – for example, the larger percentage of girls achieving the higher grades at both Key Stages 1 and 2 in reading and writing (results from the National Assembly for Wales 1999a, 1999b).

This reading of the statistics also resonates with a more sophisticated and wide-ranging analysis of the comparative performance of boys and girls at school in Wales which was undertaken by Gorard *et al.* (1999). Their study, which examined statutory assessment and examination results at KS1, 2 and 3, at GCSE and at A level, concluded that over the period studied (1992–7) the only changes in the achievement gap between boys and girls were confined to the highest levels of attainment at KS1–4 in English, Welsh and the humanities.

Why boys? Why now?

But the knowledge that boys are not well represented at the highest levels of attainment in some subjects – particularly English – does not tell us exactly *which* boys are doing badly in school. Is boys' under-achievement, as Chris Woodhead suggests and Estelle Morris implies, a problem relating to white, working-class boys? Plummer (1998) agrees in part and suggests that it is social class rather than gender or race that continues to have the single most important influence on educational attainment in Britain. She maintains that the correlation between social class and educational attainment can be seen in infant school and becomes even more marked by and post-16.

Gillborn and Mirza (2000) also recognise the impact of social class on attainment but maintain that neither social class factors nor gender differences override the influence of ethnic inequality – particularly in relation to African-Caribbean, Pakistani and Bangladeshi pupils. What is particularly worrying, they note, is that (paralleling social class) inequalities of attainment for African-Caribbean pupils become progressively greater as they move through the school system.

It would appear, then, that the impact of social class and race might have been under-emphasised in recent analyses of educational attainment. But so, too, has an acknowledgement that there has been a long-standing recognition of boys' difficulties in relation to their attainment in some subjects – particularly the languages, the arts and the humanities. In fact, within these subject areas, the gender gap is nothing new. Cohen (1998) suggests that underlying the current media panic is a mistaken view that until recently there was a 'golden age of boys' when their achievements across the curriculum outstripped those of girls. But, she claims, in the period she has been researching (from the late seventeenth century) boys have *always* 'under-achieved' in relation to the learning of languages.

Cohen (1998) points out that in the eighteenth century, for example, the greater elegance, fluency and liveliness of women's conversation compared with that of men was recognised. By the end of the eighteenth century, however, girls' quick thinking was interpreted as a sign of their inferiority while boys' 'dullness' was seen as a sign of their deep and thoughtful minds. Similarly, in the first systematic and public assessment of girls' and boys' performance (the Schools' Inquiry Commission of 1868, see Cohen 1998), not only were girls found to outperform boys but their more positive attitude towards learning was also noted. But, Cohen maintains, at this time the problem was defined not as one of boys' under-achievement but as the danger of 'overstrain' for girls. Girls' excessive conscientiousness and their almost morbid obsession with learning were castigated as unhealthy and contrasted with boys' 'breezy attitude' towards life. Cohen comments that boys' poor academic performance and their negative attitudes towards school and school-work were tolerated – even admired – as natural expressions of their rebellious, boyish ways, and seen as evidence of their real understanding and superior intellect (see also Walkerdine 1989). Even in the 1950s and 1960s, the relatively poor performance of boys in the 11+ examinations was recognised and justified in terms of boys' later development. Girls were therefore required to achieve better results than boys in this examination in order to achieve a place at selective grammar schools – 'to do otherwise would have meant that grammar schools would have been overwhelmingly populated by girls' (Epstein *et al.* 1998: 5).

So, it could be asked, why across the Western world (for example, the UK, Australia, New Zealand, Canada, the USA as well as in other European countries) is there now such a concern with the attainment of boys, particularly in relation to literacy? Does it reflect a shared realisation that, in order to compete in the global economy, literacy matters? Is it that boys' difficulties with literacy (seen as a feminine subject) were tolerated so long as boys were believed to excel in 'harder-edged' subjects such as mathematics and science? Or is it because, as Yates (1997) suggests – referring to the Australian context – that there has been a realisation that not only working-class boys but also middle-class boys are beginning to lose out to girls: for many, the problem is getting 'too close for comfort'?

It may be, of course, as Cohen (1998) suggests, that despite (or even because of) their poor attainment in tests and examinations, boys are seen as having innate, if untapped, potential. While girls' successes are neatly explained away by their obsessive attitude towards work, boys' failures are attributed to something 'external' to them. Moreover, it seems that in current explanations of boys' under-achievement in school, these external factors are related back to the 'female': essentially it is women who are to blame. This argument is built around two interrelated elements: 'missing men' and 'the feminised school'.

Who's to blame?

The missing men

I noted above that in recent years concerns have been raised about the breakdown of the 'traditional' family. One consequence of this breakdown is that many children are brought up by lone parents – usually their mothers. Young boys who do not have a male presence in their lives may take their ideas about masculinity from the often stereotypically male characters they see in cartoons, comics, television, videos and computer games: there will be no-one to demonstrate a positive model of masculinity (see Beal 1994). The problem of missing men is exacerbated by the fact that the primary school is also a female-dominated environment. The result is that boys, particularly those who are brought up by their mothers, may not be exposed 'to the "masculine" dimension of some values' – such as a more overt competitive edge (Bleach 1998: 9). Certainly, in the media, the lack of male teachers and male role models in schools has been cited as a particular cause for concern (e.g. Woodhead, reported in Lightfoot 1996). As we shall see in Chapter 2, this is considered particularly worrying in relation to boys' attainment in literacy.

At a deeper level, however, the domination of young males by female teachers and the impact that this has on boys' developing sense of masculinity has been a long-standing and widespread cause for concern (see Miller 1996). Mahoney (1998) notes that in Denmark, for example, concerns have been raised that 'school is a terrible place for boys. In school they are trapped by "The Matriarchy" and are dominated by women who cannot accept boys as they are. The women teachers mainly wish to control and suppress boys' (Kruse 1996, cited in Mahoney 1998: 44).

The feminised school

The notion that boys' under-achievement is connected to the feminisation of the curriculum, pedagogy and assessment methods has been a further recurring theme in the media. Writing in *The Times Educational Supplement*, for example, Budge (1994) suggests that women teachers may have unknowingly been moulding education and assessment to suit their gender. Concerns about teaching methods have been particularly apparent in relation to the teaching of literacy, which, it is claimed, has been dominated by (feminine) child-centred approaches that girls can tolerate but which do not suit the learning styles of boys. Stephen Byers, then schools standards minister, maintained that since the late 1970s there has been an emphasis on these unstructured teaching methods and a move away from phonics. It is this, he claims, that caused boys to fall behind in English (Lightfoot 1998), while the more formal methods of the National Literacy Strategy account for the recent rise in standards of attainment, particularly in relation to boys' reading scores (Blunkett 2000).

Moreover, it is suggested, boys' relatively poor performance in GCSE examinations is associated with the move away from the old system of O level examinations where knowledge and abstract facts – seen to favour males' cognitive styles – were prioritised. The GCSE, it is argued, has placed greater emphasis on course work,[3] open-ended tasks, context-dependent knowledge, analytical skills and verbal reasoning skills – all said to favour girls' cognitive styles (see, for example, Warrington and Younger 1997; Arnot *et al.* 1998).

Solutions?

If females and 'girl-friendly' teaching and assessment methods are to blame for boys' under-achievement, then it is unsurprising that strategies suggested to improve boys' attainment have included: the introduction of single-sex teaching; an increase in the number of male teachers and male role-models in schools; the adoption of boy-friendly teaching strategies[4] and assessment methods; the motivation of boys through the establishment of links between (predominantly male) sports, learning and literacy; and the inclusion on school reading lists of the kinds of books boys prefer. This has been reflected in headlines such as 'Single-sex Lessons Plan to Counter

Laddish Culture' (Woodward 2000); 'Labour Seeks More Male Teachers to Inspire Boys'[5] (Petre 1998); and 'Girls 1, Boys 0: Can Football Help Boys Draw Level in the Classroom? (Crace 2001).

The effectiveness of some of these strategies has been questioned. For example, Bleach (1998) and Phillips (2000) both recognise that male teachers may actually exacerbate the problem of 'laddish' behaviour amongst under-achieving boys. It could be argued, for example, that the influence of female teachers might lead to the adoption of a *less* aggressive and more flexible masculine identity (see Beal 1994). Similarly, other writers have suggested that tackling male under-achievement through emphasising boy-friendly books may also be counterproductive (Ghouri 1999) in that they may only serve to entrench the macho attitudes which caused boys to fail in the first place. As we shall see, there are no easy solutions to this problem.

Conclusions

In this chapter we have seen that through most of the last century men and women inhabited 'separate spheres' – men dominating the world of work and women the world of home. Women were encouraged to venture into the male sphere when they were needed and to assume their position as full-time mother and homemaker when they were not. But agitation by feminists for equality of opportunity, changes in women's expectations and in the traditional family structure, as well as fundamental shifts in employment patterns, have challenged males to make adjustments and to redefine masculinity. It is their difficulty with making the necessary adjustments that seems to be the problem for some men who have subsequently embraced a position of 'hyper-masculinity'. It is a commitment to the ideal of hyper-masculinity which appears to have a negative impact on boys' attitudes towards school and towards learning.

It is interesting to consider why so much emphasis has been placed on gender when it is argued that factors such as race, poverty and class may have a greater impact on educational attainment than whether one is male or female. Is it that by framing this issue as a problem of 'gender' it then leaves open the possibility of rationalising boys' under-achievement in terms of 'gender-related' issues: for example, the 'feminisation' of the curriculum, of teaching strategies and of methods of assessment, as well as the domination of schools by female teachers? Moreover, is it that it then becomes the responsibility of teachers to find a solution to this problem through, for example, changing their expectations, teaching methods and curriculum content? And if there is a genuine concern with gender equity, why is it that school and society has so easily been 'un-hitched'? Why, for example, is there is no comparable 'panic' about the position of young women in the post-school years, even though, as Treneman (1998) reminds us, 'the statistical under-achievement of boys in school is nothing compared with the statistical over-achievement of men in life'?

If we are to understand what teachers might do to raise standards – particularly standards of boys' attainment in literacy – then we need to examine how we acquire a sense of who we are as a 'gendered being' and how this might impact on children's attitudes towards and attainment in reading and writing. It is to this issue that I turn in Chapter 2.

2 Gender differences and their impact on reading and writing

Whether we are aware of it or not, stereotypes are a part of our day-to-day thinking. The world is a complicated and confusing place and, as the Equal Opportunities Commission (EOC 1992) comments, in order to make sense of it, we devise (or learn) categories that can be used to interpret what we see and what happens to us. It has often been pointed out that gender is *the* primary category by which the social world is organised (see Sheldon 1990). Gender stereotypes provide useful 'short-hand' ways of categorising our observations and experiences. They are extremely powerful – and, as we shall see, they are central to the formation of an individual's sense of self as male or female. But while they are both useful and powerful these stereotypes are also damaging in the inherent assumption that a person's gender 'automatically limits and defines his or her sphere of activity' (EOC 1992: 5).

What, then, is a gender stereotype? In simple terms, it is a set of assumptions, beliefs or expectations about what it means to be male and female. In our culture and time, the stereotypical male is often seen as aggressive, competitive, dominant, rational, ambitious, active and adventurous, while the stereotypical female is compliant, affectionate, emotional, nurturing, compassionate, talkative and gentle.

But how do these stereotypes relate to what is known of the differences between males and females? One of the key studies to explore the psychological and behavioural differences between boys and girls was undertaken by Maccoby and Jacklin in 1974. Maccoby and Jacklin consider a large body of evidence concerning sex differences and conclude, albeit tentatively, that girls appear to develop verbal abilities more rapidly than boys, while boys excel on visual-spatial ability and mathematical ability (although not in early childhood). They maintain that, compared with girls, boys are more aggressive both physically and verbally; this sex difference is found as soon as social play begins – at age two or two and a half. In addition, there is some tentative evidence to suggest that boys are more competitive and, during the pre-school years at least, more active than girls are, particularly when in the presence of other boys. When playing in single-sex groups it is claimed that boys tend to make more 'dominance attempts' than girls do, and more often try to dominate adults. Conversely, some research suggests that, compared with boys, girls are more timid, anxious and compliant to the demands and directions of adults – although not to the demands of their male and female peers. Finally, Maccoby and Jacklin state that there are indications that girls of six to ten years are more likely than boys to behave in a more nurturing way.

But are these findings accurate? And how do differences between males and females come about? In this chapter I will review some of the theories that have been proposed to explain gender differences. I will then move on to look at the ways in which gender differences are reflected in boys' and girls' reading and writing.

THE THEORIES

Essentially, theories attempting to explain gender differences can be seen to adopt different positions in relation to the nature/nurture debate – that gender differences are innate or that they are socially learned. In Chapter 1 we saw that Victorian values dominated policy and practice in education throughout much of the twentieth century. Victorian values can be linked to theories of gender as biologically determined.

Gender as biologically determined

Many researchers working in this area have explored the influence of hormones on the structure and organisation of the brain (see Kimura 1992). Those supporting this view have often claimed that the differences between men and women are due to differences in brain lateralisation.[1] Moir and Jessel (1998) maintain that, in females, language and visual-spatial skills are controlled by centres on both sides of the brain and that information flowing between the left and right hemispheres is supported by more neural connections in the corpus callossum. In males the centre controlling language is located in the left hemisphere, while that control-ling visual-spatial skills – such as the ability to picture and mentally rotate a three-dimensional image – is located in the right hemisphere. In addition, there are fewer connections supporting the flow of information between centres on either hemisphere.

This is seen as having certain consequences. Moir and Jessel (1998) indicate that the structure of the female brain means that females are more likely than males to be fluent and articulate. However, given that they have language centres in both hemispheres, females tend to use language to try and solve abstract problems that demand visual-spatial skills – this is neither efficient nor effective. Moreover, the structure of the male brain might make them less skilful verbally, but, given the lack of verbal 'inter-ference', they are more adept than females at seeing patterns and solving abstract problems.

Other than differences in verbal and visual-spatial capability, Moir and Moir (1999) cite research which suggests that the chemistry of the male brain means that, compared with females, males are more likely to be impulsive, impatient, more easily bored and derive greater pleasure from taking risks. Certainly, research has suggested that males are more aggressive than females: this has been attributed by some (e.g. Money and Ehrhardt 1972) to the prenatal exposure of males to testosterone.[2]

In addition, it is suggested that the female brain is structured (or designed!) to respond more sensitively to all sensory stimuli. Females, it is maintained, 'are equipped to receive a wider range of sensory information, to connect and relate that information with greater efficiency, to place a primacy on personal relationships, and to communicate' (Moir and Jessel 1998: 17).

And what of the 'emotional' female and 'rational' male? Moir and Jessel (1998) cite research by Sandra Witelson (1976) which found that the female brain has emotional capacities on both sides of the brain and, as noted above, a greater number of neural connections means that more information is exchanged between the left and right hemispheres. Moir and Jessel maintain that, in the female brain, the emotional side is more integrated with the verbal side and this means that females are more able to express their emotions in words. In males the centre dealing with emotion is located in the right hemisphere while, as we have seen, the centre dealing with language is in the left hemisphere. The restricted flow of information between the right and left hemisphere thus makes it more difficult for males to articulate their feelings.

Critiques

Biological theories, based on (particular) scientific evidence, sound convincing and certainly offer a neat solution to the issue of gender differences. However, a great deal of this research has been challenged by academics working in this field, particularly on the grounds of research methodology (e.g. Halpern 1992). One of the major critiques of this approach has been undertaken by Anne Fausto-Sterling (1992) in her book *Myths of Gender: Biological Theories about Women and Men*. So what are these myths?

First, Fausto-Sterling notes that many people believe that little girls begin to talk sooner than little boys do, and their greater speaking abilities make them better able to cope with the language-centred world of primary education. But is this really the case?

Fausto-Sterling notes that a small body of research does suggest that girls may talk sooner than boys but feels that 'the differences, if any, are so small relative to the variation among members of the same sex that it is almost impossible to demonstrate them in any consistent or statistically acceptable fashion' (Fausto-Sterling 1992: 26).

In addition, Fausto-Sterling challenges the conclusion that older females have superior verbal ability. Fausto-Sterling notes that when data claiming that this was the case was re-analysed using new research methods, the 'well-established' difference in verbal ability 'teeters on the brink of oblivion' (Fausto-Sterling 1992: 30).

And what of differences in visual-spatial ability? Fausto-Sterling notes that, according to Maccoby and Jacklin (1974), there are no sex-related differences in visual-spatial abilities until adolescence. Post-adolescence, the evidence of sex-related differences seems a little more convincing than for verbal abilities, although, as Maccoby and Jacklin point out, differences in spatial skill are quite small. Fausto-Sterling maintains that they are certainly too small to account for the tiny number of women who currently become professional mathematicians, architects and engineers. But if there are even small differences, do these suggest that visual-spatial abilities are biologically determined?

Fausto-Sterling (1992) notes that there is ample evidence that visual-spatial abilities are, at least in part, 'learned'. She cites as an example research which has shown that although first-grade boys did better than first-grade girls on tests designed to assess their visual-spatial skills, if given time to practice, the girls improved enough to catch up with the boys. There was, however, little change in the boys' scores. Fausto-Sterling maintains that it has been suggested that this was because boys had already honed these skills so that additional practice did not lead to improved performance. How, then, are these abilities learned?

It is recognised that boys and girls generally have different play experiences. Fausto-Sterling suggests that it is likely that typical (stereotypical?) boys' games and activities such as model construction, ball games, tree climbing, running and throwing, etc. have a significant impact on the development of certain cognitive capabilities and might account for differences in the development of spatial skills. Fausto-Sterling concludes that the developmental environment of childhood might play an important role in the attainment of specific capacities in the left and right hemispheres of the adult.

In terms of research which claims males are 'naturally' more aggressive and impulsive, Fausto-Sterling (1992) notes that, although some researchers have related this behaviour to testosterone, this research is inconclusive. She again cites anthropological research which indicates that the different roles assigned to boys and girls may have an impact on the development of aggressive behaviour. She notes that in research by Ember (1973), boys who performed feminine tasks were less aggressive than the average male. Stainton Rogers and Stainton Rogers (2001) similarly point out that in humans the relationship between testosterone and aggressive behaviour is unclear – it appears that the amount and impact of circulating testosterone in men is mediated by social and cultural factors.

For Fausto-Sterling, therefore, there is a general lack of evidence to support the view that gender differences are biologically determined. Moreover, she indicates that particular skills, capacities and characteristics demonstrated by males and females – and possibly the way in which the adult brain is structured – may have something to do with the distinctive experiences afforded to boys and girls.

A more recent analysis, however, demonstrates the difficulty of coming to any firm conclusion. Halpern (1992) reviewed studies relating to particular cognitive abilities and maintains that most literature reviews tend to underestimate the female advantage in verbal ability particularly in the pre-school and adult years. She claims that there is also evidence to support a male advantage in mathematical ability (particularly problem-solving) which emerges in adolescence and, from the end of the primary school years, an advantage for males in visual-spatial abilities – for example, spatial perception and mental rotation. But, she notes, the differences are most noticeable at the extreme ends of the ability distribution: for example, males predominate at the lower end of the verbal abilities scale and at the higher end of the mathematical abilities scale. Thus, Halpern concludes, among the middle range of abilities these differences tend to be 'smaller and more fragile' (1992: 246).[3]

It appears, therefore, that much of the research cited relating to biological origins of gender differences is tentative and inconsistent. As Connell (1995) notes, any differences 'are small compared to variation within either sex, and very small compared to differences in the social positioning of men and women' (Connell 1995: 47).

Psychoanalytic theories

Linked to the view that gender differences are biologically determined are theories that focus on the unconscious processes of mind and their impact on children's learning of the gender role. This view rests on the theories of Freud. Freud maintained that children learn to become male or female by identifying with, imitating and internalising the values of the parent of the same sex. Beal explains:

> The motivation for identifying with the same-sex parent comes from children's need to resolve the oedipal crisis, which is triggered by the discovery that boys have a penis and girls do not. The boy fears being castrated by his father, gives up his attachment to his mother, and adopts his father as a role model, while the girl becomes filled with envy, tries first to obtain a penis by becoming daddy's little girl, and then eventually accepts her mother as a role model.
>
> (1994: 59)

But given girls' mixed feelings about their mothers, this identification is not as strong as boys' identification with their fathers. According to Freud, this is the reason that females' superego – their conscience – is not as well developed as the superego of males and also accounts for the moral superiority of males and their stronger, more rigid male identity.

Chodorow (1978) reinterpreted and developed Freud's theory. She maintains that initially the mother is seen as all important in the young infant's life, and that both male and female babies identify with the mother. But, being female, the mother identifies more with a daughter than a son. Golombok and Fivush (1994) explain that this means that daughters can gradually separate from the mother while maintaining a sense of interpersonal merging. The female's self-concept thus depends on mutuality and interpersonal relatedness. Sons, on the other hand, experience the mother as 'different'. For boys, separation requires the inner repression of the feminine and the outward rejection of all that is associated with the female. The male self-concept thus depends on being an independent, autonomous individual (Golombuk and Fivush 1994).

Psychoanalytic theories have also been criticised – for example, there is little evidence that the emotional bond between mothers and daughters is different from that between mothers and sons (Golombok and Fivush 1994). In addition, Thorne (1993) argues that psychoanalytic theories cannot account for those occasions when boys and girls choose to be together. However, as Measor and Sikes (1992) point out, these theories do have the advantage of focusing on the emotional aspects of a child's life and emphasise that feelings are involved in the process of developing the gender role.

Social learning theory

Other theorists have proposed that, rather than having a biological origin, gender differences are learned through the individual's interaction within his or her 'environment'. Proponents of social learning theory, for example, maintain that children learn what it means to be male and female through two key processes: reinforcement of appropriate behaviour and the imitation of same-sex role models. Research[4] has shown, for example, that parents tend to dress their daughters and sons in different kinds of clothes, give them different toys to play with, encourage different activities and interests, interpret their behaviour differently and respond to that behaviour in different ways. From these early interactions, boys and girls are being taught powerful messages: Askew and Ross point out, for example, 'Boys are being taught to demand attention and to control situations to get what they want; whereas girls are being taught to be passive and to wait before reacting' (1988: 6).

However, the messages children receive about what is 'appropriate' behaviour may be conflicting – particularly for boys. Golombok and Fivush (1994), discussing the findings of a study by Langlois and Downs (1980), note that with boys, mothers tend to reinforce cross-gender play (play that crosses prescribed gender boundaries) while fathers reinforce gender-typed play (play that conforms to what is seen as 'normal' for a boy or girl). With girls, both mothers and fathers tend to reinforce gender-typed play, although mothers do not overtly punish cross-gender play. Golumbok and Fivush note that in the Langlois and Downs' study reinforcement was often subtle: parents did not tell their children which toys to play with but demonstrated their approval through, for example, praising or joining in with the child's play.

Golombok and Fivush (1994) point out that if the messages children receive from their parents are sometimes confusing, this is not the case with the messages they receive from their peers: for both boys and girls, same-gender play with gender-typed toys is reinforced and cross-gender play is punished. As Paechter (1998) comments, differentiation into stereo-typical gender roles is not only reinforced but also policed by the children themselves.

Of course, as in our society males generally have dominance over females, so boys have a greater investment than girls do in policing the male/female boundary. Phillips (1993) notes, 'For a girl, being more boyish means being more powerful in the world. For a boy, to be more female is to be less powerful' (1993: 59).

Millard (1994) comments that dressing in boys' clothes, playing with boys' toys and trying on a 'male role' is part of most girls' early experience. Similarly, Lloyd and Duveen (1992) note that a girl may participate in masculine activities without other people finding the behaviour odd. Boys engaging in feminine activities is not usually tolerated by peers. Dressing up in girls' clothes is only something boys can do if they make a joke out of it, otherwise it will draw adverse comments from the other children. As Paley (1984) notes, 'A boy in a frilly bedjacket expects to be laughed at, but a superhero cape on a girl creates no stir' (1984: 102).

Thorne similarly comments that the term 'tomboy' is associated with some of the positive qualities associated with the masculine, whereas the label 'sissy' suggests a failed male: 'that a boy has ventured too far into the contaminating "feminine"' (Thorne 1993: 111).

Gender and school

How far school is a force in young children's learning of gender roles has been the subject of some debate (see, for example, Connell 1989, 1996; Mac an Ghaill 1994; Skelton 1996; Swain 2000). The ways in which masculinity is constructed and demonstrated in school will be considered later in this chapter. It is important to note here, however, that according to social learning theory, children do not have to experience direct reinforcement to learn important lessons about gender. Thus a teacher's comments to a girl that 'she is looking pretty today' sends a powerful message to other children in the class about what boys and girls should attend to.

In addition, it has been suggested that school may reinforce the development of gender-related skills and abilities. Murphy and Elwood (1998) comment that, in the early years of school, boys' and girls' different interests impact on the way in which they *interact* with the school environment and so emphasise and support the development of particular skills.[5] Thus, it might be argued, the experience of school serves to amplify small, biological differences between boys and girls. Murphy and Elwood cite research by Browne and Ross (1991) who observed that even when undertaking the same activity boys and girls were using the material (in this case Lego) for different purposes: the girls made houses whereas the boys made vehicles or guns. Significantly, girls' models were used as the basis for social play whereas boys' models, which incorporated wheels and rotatable connections, encouraged them to focus on movement and balance.

Gender and children's popular culture

Of course, within our society there are many influences on boys' and girls' understandings about appropriate gender roles. Other than parents, peers and school (and, of course, children's literature), the most important of these may include children's popular culture: for example, comics, the television, video and computer games.

Marsh and Millard (2000) note that children's popular culture is permeated by violence: 'Superheroes use kicks, weapons and tricks to overcome their enemies. Computer games often involve the player "shooting up", "zapping" or blasting opponents. Toy guns and war toys encourage an obsession with death on a large scale' (2000: 26).

But it is not simply the violence that may be problematic, for media heroes are also gendered. Marsh (2000b) notes that the male superhero is strong, powerful, aggressive and usually anti-social. In his world women are either wholly evil or wholly good. Evil women are often portrayed as desexualised and physically unattractive creatures who must either be resisted or 'hunted, captured and defeated' (2000: 211). Those women who are good 'simper and whimper' and, Marsh (2000: 211) notes, are rewarded with romantic attention if they are pretty enough. Female superheroes are also active and brave (to an extent) while retaining their sexualised Barbie-like appearance. However, Marsh (2000: 211) notes, when in direct competition with a male superhero they are usually relegated to the position of 'girl'.

The ways in which media heroes – or indeed, anything else – impacts on children's understanding of the gender role is, however, far from clear. Connell (1995) indicates that a particular difficulty with social learning theory, and indeed with other theories that view gender differences as socially constructed, is that they see the body as an empty surface on which cultural meanings and cultural norms can be inscribed. This, Connell (1995) points out, is far from the case, as the surface is not featureless. He states that 'Bodies, in their own right as bodies, do matter. They age, get sick, enjoy, engender, give birth. There is an irreducible bodily dimension in experience and practice; the sweat cannot be excluded' (Connell 1995: 51).

Moreover, as Beal (1994) notes, social learning theory does not account for the wide variation within genders; boys and girls adopt different ways of being masculine and feminine and this is not necessarily related to the form of masculinity or femininity adopted by their parents. In addition, children often do things for which they know they will be punished and fail to do things which promise a reward. Beal points out that this is especially true for boys, who are reluctant to engage in feminine behaviour even if they see another boy or adult male perform this behaviour. Indeed, the whole notion of the imitation of same-sex models – that of modelling – has now been re-evaluated. The new interpretation of modelling links to cognitive developmental approaches to gender acquisition.

Cognitive developmental approaches

According to cognitive developmental theories, young children play an active role in the process of gender socialisation. Young children learn for themselves that gender is an important category in the social world and develop a gender 'identity' (Beal 1994) – a sense of themselves as being male or female. Beal notes that, having labelled themselves male or female, young children observe what is appropriate behaviour for their gender and adjust their behaviour accordingly to fit in with expectations and conventions.

This appears to accord with the notion of gender schema: the developing content and structure of gender knowledge. Golumbuk and Fivush (1994) note that, conceptually, a gender schema is quite similar to a gender stereotype. As soon as young children can accurately assign a gender label they begin to form gender schemas (or schemata) or stereotypes (see Martin and Little 1990). According to Golombok and Fivush (1994) the young child's gender schema is simple and rigid: if an individual is assigned the label 'boy' – usually on the basis of visual cues such as hairstyle and clothes (Bem 1989) – then, it is assumed, he must also have particular (stereotypically male) interests and characteristics. Moreover, as Golumbok and Fivush make clear, younger children pay more attention to information that confirms rather than challenges their schema. Gender stereotyping appears to peak at about five years of age, when children are starting school. In fact, many writers have supported the view that gender-typed behaviour is particularly significant in the early years of school. Paley (1984) notes, for example that:

> Kindergarten is a triumph of sexual self-stereotyping. No amount of adult subterfuge or propaganda deflects the five-year-old's passion for

segregation by sex. They think they have invented the differences between boys and girls and, as with any new invention, must prove it works.

(Paley 1984: ix)

Beal (1994) suggests that many pre-school children conform to gender stereotypes because they do not really understand what makes someone male or female. Once they realise that biology rather than visual appearance or behaviour is significant – in Kohlberg's (1966) terms they have achieved gender constancy – they become more tolerant of deviations from 'expected' gender roles. Gender stereotypes eventually decline when children realise that many gender role behaviours are social conventions rather than moral imperatives (Beal 1994). In terms of gender schema theory, then, children gradually develop more detailed and more complexly organised knowledge, first about their own and then the other gender (Golombok and Fivush 1994).

Feminist post-structuralist theory

Those who adopt a feminist post-structuralist perspective also reject the notion that gender differences are the result of the child being passively socialised. These theorists argue that social values and norms cannot be *imposed* on children as the individual and the social world are not separate entities; rather they are 'interdependent and mutually constructing' (MacNaughton 2000). In other words, the concepts of masculinity and femininity are not inherent in individuals but inherent and structural properties of society itself (Davies 1989). Through learning about these structures children learn to position themselves correctly as male or female: what are deemed to be appropriate, normal and possible ways of thinking, feeling, behaving.

I noted above that Connell (1995) maintains that the body is 'inescapable' in the construction of masculinity. Bronwyn Davies (1989) similarly suggests that positioning is not just a conceptual process but a physical one as well – the body takes on knowledge of being male or female through its practices – for example, dress, hairstyle, posture, movement, etc. Moreover, as we shall see, language also plays a crucial role in this learning: as Davies comments, 'language also provides the tools and the materials with which the social structure is created and maintained' (1989: 1). In making sense of their worlds, young children actively make use of categories – binary pairs such as good/bad, strong/weak and pretty/ugly. One of the most significant of these binary pairs relates to gender – male/female. I noted earlier that Sheldon (1990) points out that gender is seen as *the* primary category by which the social world is ordered and organised. Davies (1989) comments that children take up their maleness and femaleness through learning the discursive practices in which all people are positioned as either male or female. Indeed, the division of people into males and females is so fundamental to our understanding of identity that it is often understood as a natural fact rather than something that is learned (Davies 1993). Children not only learn about these categories and the practices that arise from them, they also make an emotional investment in getting their practices 'right'. This investment Davies refers to as 'patterns of desire' – she claims that children take up as their own the particular patterns of desire relevant to their gender and what are seen as 'proper' ways of being male and female.

But within the binary pair these categories are not equal: Paechter (1998) comments that one is given priority over the other or is even seen as the negative of the other. In terms of gender, as I noted above, we live in a society that (still) is patriarchal: males hold power, and, in most contexts, masculinity is prized above femininity. Within most discourses,[6] therefore, 'male' is positioned in dominance over 'female'. But when individuals feel that they have been positioned as powerless this may be resisted. An example of this is given by Walkerdine (1989) who describes a nursery classroom where children are playing hospitals. Initially the boy takes on the role of (powerful) doctor and the girl is positioned in a supportive role as the nurse. But, as Walkerdine, explains, the girl manages to convert the context of the play to a domestic setting. Rather than being the subservient nurse, the girl is now positioned as the controlling woman in the home and so has power over the boy.

While a consideration of our own experiences reveals that there are many possible ways of 'being' male and female, the child learns that, within our society, there are dominant views of what is seen as normal and desirable. Connell (1995) notes that for boys, 'hegemonic' masculinity (associated with the stereotypical male or 'lad') is the most exalted of these and serves to marginalise or subordinate others.

For most males, however, hegemonic masculinity is an *idea* of masculinity (Davies 1989) it is not something that is lived out in its entirety any more than females live out its opposite: 'emphasised' femininity (Connell 1987, 1995). And even within the different forms of masculinity there are many ways of 'being', given that multiple discourses intersect in any individual life (Connell 1995). Post-structuralists recognise that in reality human beings are more than simple stereotypes. Rather, our subjectivity – who we are and how we understand ourselves, consciously and unconsciously (MacNaughton 2000) – is complex, multi-layered, often contradictory and constantly changing (Davies 1989).

Gender and language

As I noted above, poststructuralists such as MacNaughton (2000) see language as the key to how we construct our subjectivity. MacNaughton maintains that language 'constructs how we think, feel, act, desire and speak' and also 'constitutes what we believe is normal, right and desirable' (2000: 97).

Since the mid-1970s, many feminists have pointed out that sexism is embedded within our language structure and usage. Dale Spender (1985), for example, argues forcefully that the male superiority/female inferiority dichotomy is a principle encoded in our language which thus structures and maintains the subordination of females. Spender notes, for example, how women are silenced – are made invisible – by the use of the term 'man' (and he) to represent both men and women. Spender refers to the work of Schulz (1975) who points out that in the English language not only are there more positive words for males than females but that many of the negative words for females have no semantic male equivalent. Schulz maintains that over time words linked with the female, or words which have been shifted into the female sphere, have systematically acquired negative (and often sexual) connotations: consider, for example, master/mistress, king/queen, sir/madam. This process Schulz sees as a semantic rule in a society that constructs male supremacy.

In addition, it is argued that males and females use language in different ways in order to signal membership of a particular gender group (see, for example, Graddol and Swann 1989). Robin Lakoff (1975) identi-fied a set of features which she maintains occur more frequently in women's speech than in men's speech and thus could be referred to as 'women's language'. Lakoff maintains that this language gives the impres-sion that women are polite, tactful, hesitant and lacking in authority. This resonates with Walkerdine's (1989) comment that in her research throughout all age groups the most desirable characteristics of girls were seen as 'nice', kind and helpful. Tannen (1990) maintains that males, on the other hand, tend to use conversations as an arena for negotiating and maintaining status – their performances are intended to get attention and to keep it. Thus, for men, jokes, storytelling and the imparting of informa-tion are important features of their talk. Sheldon (1990) also points to research (for example, Maltz and Borker 1982; Gilligan 1987) that suggests that in their speech females tend to be collaborative, connected and empathetic whereas males tend to be competitive, independent and adversarial.

Gender and school

One theme that appears to be common to all theories that view gender differences as socially constructed is that males and females demonstrate their gender in a multitude of ways: for example, through attitude, body posture, behaviour, dress, language. How then is masculinity displayed in school? One way, it seems, is through appearing 'tough'. Boys need to establish themselves as members of the powerful cultural group – particu-larly in a context where the person with day-to-day power over them is usually female – and showing their commitment to an ideal of hegemonic masculinity is one way of achieving this aim. Epstein (1998) comments that, in the primary school, of all the insults that can be thrown at a boy the worst is being called a 'girl'.

But a commitment to the idea of heterosexual relationships is also important in being seen as a 'real' and 'normal' male. Skelton (1997) notes how, in response to an unfamiliar female teacher, even boys of six and seven adopted sexualised bodily postures and adopted confrontational and aggressive behaviours. Benjamin (2001) reports a contamination game which was often played by the boys in her study, in which the chaser would be gay and pass 'gayness' on to whichever player he caught. 'Macho Man', Benjamin states, 'was the antithesis of all things gay and girlie' (2001: 45).

In her exploration of children's gender and sexual identities in the final year of primary school, Renold (2000) illustrates how sexuality and, in particular, heterosexuality is part of the everyday experience of primary school children. Many boys she observed also demonstrated their masculinity through heterosexual performances. For boys of this age, however, 'going out with girls' created particular conflicts and anxieties. Proximity to girls could confirm boys' heterosexuality. But given their need to reject females and the feminine, it could also lead to jibes about homosexuality. Renold notes that one way of responding to this difficulty was for boys to assert their heterosexuality through misogyny and homophobia.

Mucking around

As I noted in Chapter 1, having a laugh and adopting a negative attitude towards school and school-work are part of the culture of laddish behaviour. Epstein (1998: 98) maintains that her research supported the view that one of the dominant notions of (hegemonic) masculinity in many schools was the avoidance of academic work, or at least the avoidance of the appearance of working. This is not just associated with boys of secondary school age; even in primary schools Epstein (1998) noted the bullying and harassment through homophobic name-calling of boys who worked hard. If boys are finding academic work difficult, it may be understandable that gaining the admiration of their peers for being the 'class clown' is more appealing than risking being seen as a swot or a failure.

How then, do boys who are academic high-achievers demonstrate their masculinity in school? This is problematic and, as I have indicated above, many of the high-achieving boys appear to be subject to homophobic abuse. What is particularly disturbing is the suggestion that some teachers may be complicit in this – in Mac an Ghaill's (1994) study, for example, a number of teachers as well as students viewed the academic achievers as effeminate. Those male achievers who *do* manage to maintain their male-ness may do so through publicly resisting the authority of the teacher. But, it appears, boys have available to them another way of demonstrating their masculinity in school: through sport and, in particular, through football.

Masculinity and sport

In his study of Year 6 boys, Swain (2000) found that football was a key signifier of successful masculinity. This is not surprising given that foot-ball, as Swain (2000) notes, can be seen as the pinnacle of hegemonic, heterosexual masculinity, communicating ideals of fitness, strength, competition, power and domination. Swain argues that, through football, boys were learning how to use their bodies to demonstrate strength and competence; they attempted to look like and emulate their professional football heroes and, in so doing, practised being men. Playing football had an almost tribal appeal and the football lads excluded girls as well as subordinate groups of boys who were feminised through homophobic name-calling. Football was very competitive: Swain points out that for these boys, winning was everything and not winning was seen as signifying stereotypical 'feminine' traits such as dependence and vulnerability.

Girls and gender identity

Of course girls are also subject to pressure to display their gender identity and, like hegemonic masculinity, its opposite – 'emphasised femininity' (Connell 1987, 1995) – is often used as an ideal on which behaviour is modelled and against which behaviour is judged. This has been noted from the beginning of the school years: Ochsner (2000), for example, notes that emphasised femininity was displayed by the 5- and 6-year-old girls in her study through, for example, their body movements, clothes and through the discourse of 'make-up': make-up was a theme that emerged in the chil-dren's talk, actions, drawing and writings. Ochsner notes: 'Throughout my study, girls were documented using their knowledge of make-up to posi-tion themselves as objects of desire and in relation to hegemonic masculinity' (2000: 212).

Renold (2000) similarly notes that, for many of the Year 6 girls in her study, femininity depended on heterosexual desirability and this was displayed through, for example, the shape and size of their bodies, the clothes they wore and their engagement in discussions of 'fancying', 'going out with' and 'dumping'. Girls who did participate in what Renold calls the 'flirty fashion' discourse but chose to wear sporty or comfy clothes were accepted only if they demonstrated their heterosexuality in other ways – for example, through having heterosexual 'relationships'. Those girls who did not demonstrate this commitment were at risk of being ridiculed as 'non-girls', 'weirdos' and 'boys'.

Theories of gender acquisition – a summary

Having explored a number of theories which attempt to explain gender differences, we are left with a complex and confusing picture. In one sense, these theories are looking at different aspects of the same whole – or looking at the same whole from different perspectives. In another, they propose very different explanations for the causes of gender differences (and the gender gap) and thus indicate very different solutions.

It is interesting to speculate why the notion of gender as biologically determined – one of the most contentious theories – has gained so much support in the media and popular press in recent years. Is it that it provides support for the view that the current difficulties experienced by males are, at least in part, due to the disintegration of the traditional family with man as head of household and woman as full-time home-maker? Has this theory been seized on in an attempt (yet again) to encourage women to adopt the role of full-time mother and home-maker?

Certainly, some proponents of this view suggest that the current crisis in masculinity is based on our lack of understanding – and even rejection – of the traditional roles of man as hunter-gatherer and woman as nurturer and carer. Differences in the organisation of our brains, it is argued, are the result of natural selection, based on the needs of the hunter-gatherer societies – our brains are essentially like those of our ancestors of over 50,000 years ago (Kimura 1992). It is our resistance to the adoption of our 'natural' roles which has resulted in such chaos, confusion and unhappiness for men and women (Pease and Pease 1998).

GENDER AND LITERACY

Common to all these theories is a recognition that 'gender' has a profound impact on the way in which individuals think, speak and act, and on their sense of self – who they are in the world. Moreover, whichever perspective is adopted, it is likely that, to a greater or lesser extent, gender will influence attitudes towards literacy, the development of literacy skills as well as preferences in reading and writing.

As we have seen, those upholding a view of gender as biologically determined argue that, by virtue of the structure of their brains, girls are 'naturally' advantaged and boys disadvantaged in relation to activities based on language. Moreover, it has been suggested that, within our culture, literacy is constructed as a passive, 'female-appropriate' activity. It is pointed out, for example, that children are usually taught to read by their mothers or female teachers, while girls are more likely than boys to be given books as presents and are more often portrayed as readers in the illustrations in children's books (Millard 1997).

Those who subscribe to psychoanalytic theories of gender construction, therefore, might see boys' rejection of literacy as a way of repressing and separating themselves from all that is female in order to identify with and establish themselves as male. Moreover, advocates of social learning theory might argue that, through reinforcement and reward, boys learn that literacy is not an appropriate activity for them. A rejection of reading and writing is therefore used by boys as a way of demonstrating their male identity (cognitive developmental approaches) and as a way of positioning themselves as a 'normal', hegemonic, heterosexual male (post-structuralist feminist theory).

All these theories, then, indicate that, compared with girls, boys are likely to 'under-achieve' in language and literacy. It is therefore important to take a closer look at the differences between girls' and boys' attitudes towards and preferences in reading and writing. Do these also reflect gender differences?

Reading

We know that girls have a more positive attitude towards reading (Hall and Coles 1999) and read more than boys do (Barrs 1993; White 1996) – although, as Hall and Coles (1997) point out, this has been the case for many decades. Moreover, boys and girls like to read different kinds of material: it is generally agreed that girls are more likely to buy books and magazines than boys (Hall and Coles 1999) and that females read more fiction than males and males read more non-fiction than females (Barrs 1993; White 1996; Hall and Coles 1999). Moreover, boys and girls like to read about different things: from an early age it has been found that while girls like stories about families, boys prefer stories about boys (Appleyard 1991), adventure, humour and football (Hall and Coles 1997). Similarly, boys favour comics such as the *Beano* (Hall and Coles 1997) as well as those with 'themes of violence and terror' (White 1996), tabloid newspapers, football magazines (Hall and Coles 1997, 1999) and hobby magazines (White 1996). It appears, however, that the popularity of comics decreases as children get older – particularly with girls (Hall and Coles 1997, 1999) – with newspapers and magazines beginning to displace comics in Year 6 (Davies and Brember 1993).

Reading at home and at school

Mallett (1997) notes that in her study children chose very different genres in the home compared with at school, with gender differences being more marked in the home setting. Mallett found that both the Year 6 boys and girls enjoyed listening to and reading fiction in school. At home, however, the boys' reading choices were related to entertainment – they were more likely than girls to specify ghost and horror stories as well as comics and sports magazines. Girls also read for entertainment at home but they mentioned a wider range of genres. These findings have been reflected in other studies. For example, Osmot and Davis's small-scale study of children's reading (1987, cited in Barrs 1993) found that most girls were satisfied with the choice of books available to them in the classroom reading corners. Their reading at home was not significantly different from their reading in school. Boys were less satisfied. At home they read different kinds of material – comics and media-related fiction bought in newsagents rather than bookshops. They would have liked some of this kind of reading to be available in school. Similarly, Millard (1994) notes that several of the boys in her study suggested that they would like to read— computer magazines and other magazines related to their hobbies in independent reading time. In addition, they complained that other kinds of books such as Superhero or Transformer stories were not accepted as appropriate school reading matter.

Reading books differently

But, as Minns (1993) notes, it is not only that boys prefer different texts from those enjoyed by girls but that they may read books differently: boys may, for example, adopt a view of reading which is about 'finding out'. Minns refers to the reading of three 10-year-old boys. Minns notes that one of these boys, Clayton, interrogates the text (*Charlotte's Web*) in a way that keeps his feet securely in the world of facts. Minns comments that it is 'as if Clayton is transforming what could be a totally aesthetic experience into a factual exchange of dates, and making them part of his theory of how the world works' (1993: 65).

Minns notes that what appears to underpin the focus of Clayton's reading choices is the influence of his father – he models his own reading behaviour on his father's reading style and preferences. If children's reading preferences are influenced through the observation and imitation of appropriate gender models (social learning theory) then it may be of significance that Osmot (1987) found that children perceived their mothers as reading mainly fiction whereas their fathers were perceived to read newspapers, information books and documents brought back from work. Millard (1997) also notes that reading at home was perceived by boys and girls as an activity closely associated with the female members of the family. The reading they undertook with their fathers was reading to find out about computer games and searching Teletext for sports results.

But there may be other differences in the way girls and boys approach texts. Sarland (1991), for example, claims that girls make connections between their reading and their own lived experiences – they find the text in themselves (Barrs 1993). Boys, on the other hand, find themselves in the text – they project themselves into the stereotyped characters of their preferred fictions. In other words, as Barrs (1993) indicates, boys appear to choose texts they know are likely to legitimise their experiences and support their view of themselves while girls seek to extend who they are through taking into themselves experiences that are very different from their own.

I noted earlier in this chapter that boys' gender identity is much more rigid and narrow than that of girls and this seem to be the point that Barrs (1993) and Sarland (1991) are making here in relation to children's reading. As with their gender identity, girls appear willing to enter male 'territory' and to learn about male as well as female experiences. Sarland (1991) maintains, for example, that while the (teenage) boys in his study tended to read for action, girls read for action *but also* for relationships and characterisation. Girls did not reject 'boys' books' although they read these books differently from boys. Boys, on the other hand, maintained that they would not consider reading books that dealt with the female experience – books were rejected because of the content, title, even the picture on the cover (see Barrs 1993).

Writing

A great deal of research has also examined and compared boys' and girls' writing of stories. Burgess Macey (1992, cited in Barrs 1993) found that the stories of girls often featured domestic or family themes. Similarly, Paley (1984) comments that in every year girls begin with stories that centre around 'good little families', while others have noted that girls' stories are often set within the tradition of fairy tales (see White 1990). As part of the National Writing Project (NCC 1990) young girls were found to write stories with happy endings about birthday parties, princesses and marriage, while older girls' stories, it is claimed, typically feature love and romance as their ultimate life goals (Gilbert 1989).

It is maintained that girls' stories tend to consist of a single complication and resolution (Marsh 1998), and they often include a great deal of dialogue and description (e.g. White 1990; Burgess Macey, cited in Barrs 1993). Through this dialogue and description, girls often introduce emotion into the plot and focus the attention on the relationships between characters (NCC 1990). Burgess Macey (1992, cited in Barrs 1993) claims that girls tend to write in the third person – they generally don't write about themselves as the main character. Moreover, when girls do create heroes these tend to be placed in a passive role, subordinate to other characters and reliant on the help of others (NCC 1990).

Boys, on the other hand, have been found to write aggressive, bloodthirsty stories (NCC 1990), often about authority and control and containing superheroes and bad guys (e.g. Paley 1984). Minns (1991) suggests that boys' stories are often fantasies of power and domination. The NCC (1990) found that boys' stories tended to include an assertive, central character and, compared with girls' stories, a stronger sense of place and spatial awareness, often concentrating on the size of things:

biggest being best! Burgess Macey (1992, cited in Barrs 1993) comments that the boys in her study generally wrote in the first person or wrote the story about themselves. In addition, they appeared in their stories in heroic roles, sometimes associated with media heroes.

Millard (1997) also notes that boys draw heavily on film and television narrative in their story-writing, and they tend to make use of the language of the comic books and cartoons they enjoy (White 1990; Marsh 1998). Unsurprisingly, then, boys' stories tend to feature serialisation: their main character – the hero – being reborn to take part in a number of adventures (Marsh 1998). Moreover, boys' stories are often action-packed (Burgess Macey 1992, cited in Barrs 1993) with feelings being much less apparent than in stories written by girls (NCC 1990). They also make less use of dialogue than girls do, except where there is a need to move the action along (Burgess Macey 1992, cited in Barrs 1993).

In relation to boys' writing, then, the significance of – and possibly the obsession with – confronting and triumphing over an evil aggressor is noted by many writers. Jordan (1995) explores this idea further and maintains that the stories young boys write (as well as the pictures they paint and the games they play) are often based on the 'warrior' discourse: narratives that depict the male as warrior, knight errant and superhero. Similarly, Thomas (1997) argues that boys' narratives celebrate the mythic potency of the man whose decisive and violent acts triumph over the forces of evil. He claims that the complexities of intention and morality, and of human fallibility, have no place in heroic struggles with demons – it is 'contest without context' (Thomas 1997: 26). Thomas appears to capture the essential characteristics of boys' writing in his statement that:

> If narrative is a vehicle, then boys like driving it for reasons which have nothing to do with carrying anything, or with passenger comfort.
>
> With boys, it's all maximum revs. Each action incident is another gear change and acceleration. It makes for a bumpy journey, with lots of screeching tyres, hilltop chases and spectacular crashes. Narrative travel, boy-style, is not restful, and tells us nothing about the terrain. … As narrative drivers, they see the road ahead as their own, an invitation to celebrate solo potency, to put themselves or their character in the driving seat.
>
> (Thomas 1997: 24–5)

Conclusion

I noted above that, on the basis of the many theories which attempt to explain gender differences, it is understandable that boys have difficulties with literacy; that compared with girls they 'under-achieve'. Girls are likely to benefit from their more positive attitude towards reading and writing. Moreover, girls' practices and preferences appear to be more in keeping with what is seen as 'legitimate' in terms of school literacy: for example, girls' liking of fiction rather than non-fiction, and their emphasis on description and relationships rather than action and aggression. In addition, I noted that in their stories boys tend to draw on film and television narrative and to make use of the language of cartoons. Millard (1997, cited in Marsh and Millard 2000) points out that, given that conventional narratives are often required for assessment purposes, this can be to their disadvantage.

But are the advantages for girls as clear-cut as this analysis might suggest? Literacy may be associated with the 'feminine' but at the same time, through their titles and content, stories may convey messages about the relative importance of males and females in society and what are seen as appropriate gender roles. Ernst (1995) notes, for example, that in her study of the titles of over 2,000 children's books published in the USA in the early 1990s, males were clearly represented 640 times and females only 354 times. In addition, Ernst (1995) found that amongst the biographies of heroes and famous people written for children, there were at least twice as many books about men than about women. Ernst argues that this may demonstrate to young children 'that men are more important than women and that men do more things that warrant being written about than women do. This imbalance also results in girls having fewer role models than boys' (1995: 72).

Of course, as Ernst points out, having a female gender tag in the title does not mean that the main character is portrayed in a positive or non-stereotypical way. Books may only serve to confirm (to girls as their main readers) the appropriateness of particular gender-typed behaviour and attitudes. Jett-Simpson and Masland (1993), for example, suggest that (in keeping with the content of girls' stories) 'female story characters typically attain their goals because they are helped by others, but males achieve as a result of their own efforts' (1993: 104).

Similarly, Fox (1993) asks:

> Girls can do anything, or so we are told. They can be anything. They can feel anything. Why is it, then, that in children's literature they are still portrayed more often than not as acted upon rather than active? As nurturers rather than adventurous? As sweetness and light rather than thunder and lightning? As tentative, careful decision makers rather than wild, impetuous risk takers? Could children's literature be partly to blame for the fact that we grown-up girls have been denied in our womanhood the excitement and power so readily available to boys and grown-up boys?'
>
> (1993: 84–5)

Does girls' gendered writing – about love, dependency and 'happy ever after' – only serve to confirm and embed the idea that males are more powerful than females? And does boys' writing about power and domination reinforce their views about the status of males in society? These are issues that will be pursued in later chapters. In Chapter 3, however, I turn to a consideration of the aims and methods of this project.

3 The project

Methods and issues

In Chapter 1 I noted that the New Labour government has warned that in respect of poor standards – for example, boys' under-achievement in literacy – 'poverty is no excuse' (Davies 2000: 16). This belief can be linked to the School Improvement movement and, in particular, to the School Effectiveness movement. As we shall see, however, the link between effective schools and equity is not straightforward. On the one hand, School Effectiveness came about in response to the recognition that home background *did* matter: that it had a far greater influence on a child's background than did the school (Mortimore 1998). In order to ascertain whether particular schools were more effective than others and what characteristics these schools possessed there was therefore a need to identify the impact of the home background. On the other hand, it is argued (Jackson, D. 1998) that the language of School Effectiveness can mask the broader and more significant issues of gender equity and social justice – in this case through its emphasis on *boys'* disadvantage and, specifically, on boys' disadvantage in relation to the internal school organisation. Thus, whatever the complexities of boys' under-achievement and its intersection with poverty, socio-economic grouping or race, the focus of the School Effectiveness movement is firmly fixed on strategies that teachers can use to raise boys' standards of literacy within school.

So how does School Effectiveness relate to School Improvement? Mortimore (1998) notes that in recent years, given the significance placed on student outcomes, it is unsurprising that the goals of School Improvement have begun to move closer to those of School Effectiveness. School Improvement, in essence, is about change within schools with the ultimate aim of being able to accomplish educational goals more effectively. The responsibility for change lies not with those outside the school but with the school itself (Stoll and Fink 1996). Mortimore (1998) maintains that there are three broad phases to this change process: initiation (the process leading to the decision to change); implementation (putting innovations into practice); and institutionalization (whether or not these innovations become embedded in ongoing practice).

How then can School Improvement be supported? Mortimore adapts the work of Joyce (1991) who refers to a number of different 'doors' – some of which are being opened from the inside and others opened by those outside school (e.g. action following an inspection, involvement in an LEA-led project). Among the internally opening doors are:

- *collegiality*: 'the development of cohesive and professional relationships within and beyond schools and efforts to improve the culture of the schools';
- *research*: 'the use of research findings on school and classroom effectiveness and School Improvement';
- *self-evaluation*: 'the collection and analysis of school and student data, action research in classrooms and staff appraisal';
- *teaching and learning*: 'the study, discussion and development of teaching skills and strategies'; and
- *partnerships*: 'activities and projects that involve parents, community representatives and agencies, LEAs, business and industry, higher education, TECs and educational consultants.

(Mortimore 1998: 262)

The idea of School Improvement through the opening of internal doors was a key principle driving this project. In this chapter I briefly consider the broad framework of action research before focusing in more detail on a number of research methods and research issues. While in a sense I am telling my own story in this chapter, it is hoped that a discussion of these methods and issues will be of relevance to teachers wanting to undertake school-based research. A consideration of the benefits and limitations of the teachers' own research projects is included in later chapters. First, however, it is important to describe the context for this research.

The school context

At the time of the project the school had approximately 280 pupils on roll, 35 per cent of whom received free school meals. In recent years SATs results had reflected the national picture and boys' under-achievement in literacy had been identified by the head teacher (Dave) as a cause for concern. Indeed, it was Dave who initiated the support of the University and the LEA in order to explore this issue in greater depth. The research thus involved collaboration between the staff of this school, lecturers from the Department of Education and the LEA English Adviser. It is important to emphasise here that the teachers in this school had been interested in this issue for some time and had already implemented a number of positive strategies: for example, taking children to a bookshop and encouraging them to choose books for the school library; inviting children's authors (particularly men) to run writing workshops, etc.

The project

As a first phase of this research all members of staff – that is, three male teachers (including the head teacher) and eight female teachers – were interviewed individually. While the aim of these interviews was to explore teachers' perceptions of boys' difficulties with writing, the teachers also made reference to other aspects of literacy and to girls' perceived difficulties and achievements.

Having examined teachers' perceptions of children's difficulties there was a felt need to ascertain their actual difficulties. In a second study, then, teachers identified a sample of six children in their class (three boys and three girls) from the top, middle and lower ability ranges. All writing undertaken by this sample group was collected over a period of six weeks. This was categorised under the following headings: narrative, report, argument, persuasion, poem, instruction, explanation, play script, letter, journal and non-specific. The writing was analysed by the head teacher, by the LEA English adviser and by the teachers themselves and the findings discussed at a project meeting. At a later stage, the teachers also made a written record of their responses. I analysed the children's writing as well – that is, their stories – to see how far children's gender identities were demonstrated in these narratives.

In the third phase of the research, I explored boys' difficulties with literacy through talking to the children themselves – I wanted to find out what they had to say about the teaching and learning of literacy in school. The children – that is the six children from each class whose work had been analysed in the second phase of this research – appeared happy (in some cases eager) to leave their classrooms in order to participate in these discussions. The nine group interviews, which were audio-taped, took place in a withdrawal room and each interview lasted approximately 20 minutes.

Following these three studies, the teachers individually and collaboratively devised and piloted strategies designed to improve aspects of their practice. For many of the teachers this was their first attempt at school-based research and they saw it as a rehearsal for the next year when they were to be part of an extensive LEA project focused on improving literacy.

If the context for this project was that of School Improvement then the approach adopted by the teachers was initially characterised as one of 'action research'. Indeed, the first three phases of the research were viewed not as separate studies but as part of an overall collection of baseline data; as an action research team (of which I formed a part), we were attempting to gain an understanding – to gain evidence – of the current situation.

Action research

The nature and purposes of action research have been interpreted in many different ways (see Hopkins 1993). Elliott (1991) maintains that an essential precondition of action research is, 'A felt need on the part of the practitioners to change, to innovate' (1991: 53). Moreover, Elliott suggests that one of the key features of this approach is its emphasis on improving practice rather than on producing knowledge. McKernan (1996) maintains that 'Action research is carried out by practitioners seeking to improve their understanding of events, situations and problems so as to increase the effectiveness of their practice' (1996: 4).

Other researchers have claimed that action research is often collaborative (Hitchock and Hughes 1995), focuses on practical problems (Oja and Smulyan 1989), and is systematic and critical (McNiff *et al.* 1996).

The action research process is often described as cyclical or as an ongoing spiral moving from an initial plan which may include the collection of evidence, to action (trying out particular strategies), to observation (monitoring progress and collecting evidence), to reflection (evaluating the effectiveness of the strategy/ies). This leads to a revised plan and modified action which is then observed and reflected on. It is this process that provided a broad framework for teachers when pursuing their individual and collaborative projects.

But the action research approach is not without its critics. Hopkins (1993) for example, has concerns that this approach may be seen as functionalist rather than emancipatory and that the steps and cycles may be constraining and inhibit independent action. Moreover, Hopkins is concerned that the emphasis on 'improvement' could suggest a deficit model of professional development: that something is wrong and needs to be corrected. Rather than referring to 'action research', therefore, Hopkins prefers to talk about teachers' 'classroom research'. Hopkins (1993: 57–60) outlines six principles for such research:

- it should not interfere with or disrupt teachers' primary job of teaching;
- the method of data collection should not be too demanding on teachers' time;
- the methodology should be rigorous – reliable enough for teachers to formulate hypotheses and develop strategies applicable to their classroom situations;
- teachers should be committed to the research problem undertaken;
- teacher researchers should pay close attention to ethical procedures;
- classroom research should adopt a 'classroom exceeding' perspective: that is, it should relate to a whole-school vision and approach.

What, then, were the main research methods used in this project? And what issues emerged from the use of these methods?

Methods and issues

It is important here to emphasise that in this research project I adopted a dual role: I was both 'researcher' and 'colleague/collaborator'. As 'researcher' I was an 'outsider' – I had a responsibility to interpret teachers' comments as accurately and sensitively as possible and to provide teachers with accessible and constructive feedback. But as a member of the action research team I was an 'insider'. It was not simply that I wanted to understand teachers' viewpoints, but that I wanted us, as a *team*, to arrive at a 'shared understanding' of the situation. Moreover, I was also an 'insider' in that I wanted to examine not only the teachers' understandings and beliefs but my own understandings and beliefs as well. Through involvement in this project I was trying to gain a better understanding of my own values in relation to gender.

Values

This dual role proved difficult in relation to the notion of 'improvement' of practice. As Dadds (1995) states, 'Improvement implies values, and has an ethical orientation' (1995: 175). In earlier chapters I have noted that issues surrounding gender as well as teaching and learning are not value-neutral. What counts as 'improvement', therefore, will necessarily depend on the particular perspective – the values, attitudes and beliefs – of the 'assessor'. For example, even if, as part of this research, boys' attainment in literacy improved according to SATs results, could this be described as an authentic 'improvement'? Did it matter how this improvement was brought about? What account, for example, would need to be taken of the impact of teachers' changed actions on girls' attainment?

The issue of 'values' – that is, my own values in respect of gender and literacy – became increasingly visible to me as I worked with the teachers and pupils. For example, I realised through talking to the teachers that as a female my sympathies lay with the girls – I felt more at ease with their ways of talking and behaving and more connected with their experiences and difficulties. Indeed, on several occasions I had to make a conscious effort to see the situation from the boys' perspectives. I also recognised that, in line with feminist post-structuralist theory, I (that is, how I saw and felt about myself) was a mass of tensions and contradictions. These realisations, which I describe further in Chapter 8, were not entirely comfortable!

Interview

In the first and third phases of this study, the data was collected through semi-structured interview (see, for example, Hammersley and Atkinson 1983; Keats 1997); I drew up a provisional outline of issues and questions which I could use as prompts in my conversations with the interviewees. In keeping with qualitative research, interviews were seen as dynamic, with both myself and the respondents reacting to the questions, the answers, and to each other (Keats 1997). For example, I acknowledged that issues such as gender, age, perceptions of status and the like would impact on how questions were asked, answered and interpreted (see, for example, Measor 1985). Moreover, I acknowledged that both myself and the respondents were driven, at least to an extent, to protect our self-image and needs.

In the course of the interviews, while I did not restrict myself to a single mode of questioning (Hammersley and Atkinson 1983), I occasionally made use of more direct questions which allowed me to probe or to clarify misunderstandings. I recognised that where the questioning became too deep or focused on sensitive issues, this often resulted in avoidance tactics. Comments therefore had to be carefully phrased; I had to judge as the interview progressed how far I could 'go' with each respondent. In addition, I found that in order to gain 'rich' data it was ineffective to ask questions about generalised issues relating to teaching and learning or to ask teachers to discuss their experiences in what, to them, were unnatural theoretical terms (Ely *et al.* 1997). I found that abstract non-specific questions produced neat textbook answers. If I wanted to 'unearth' the richness and complexity of teachers' thinking it was necessary instead to ground questions in discussions of classroom practice.

Interviews were not just carried out individually but with groups of teachers as well. Group interviews have been found to have certain advantages and disadvantages. For example, Hammersley and Atkinson (1983) maintain that group interviews have the advantage of making the interview situation less strange for interviewees and thus are less of a strain. Fontana and Frey argue that group interviews are 'inexpensive, data rich, flexible, stimulating to respondents, recall aiding, and cumulative and elaborative, over and above individual responses' (1994: 365).

Watts and Ebbutt (1987) suggest, however, that group interviews are of little use in allowing personal matters to emerge. This did not appear to be a difficulty in this research. The teachers in this school knew me well and appeared willing to discuss their frustrations, fears and failures as well as testing out their tentative understandings and sharing their successes. Moreover, besides the practical and organisational advantages, through discussing and contrasting their responses to my questions, individual group members were able to clarify and evaluate their own perspectives. On occasions, however, it was difficult to tell whether certain individuals were persuaded to go along with the majority view; whether, if they had been interviewed individually, their responses would have been different.

Researching children's views

Interviews were also undertaken with groups of children. When interviewing children, particularly young children, it is considered vital to think carefully about how questions are phrased (see Greig and Taylor 1999). I was aware that being seen as a more powerful adult, the children (particularly the girls) might try to work out from the way a question was worded what was the expected or right answer.

Hopkins (1993) also notes that when an 'outsider' is used to interview pupils they may be reluctant to divulge information. On the other hand, he notes, the children may be more candid with an 'outsider'. This certainly was my experience: as I had visited the school over several years and was therefore a 'familiar face', the children appeared comfortable talking to me. At the same time, recognising that I was not a teacher and therefore within the school context had no real status or power, they did not appear to be attempting to conceal their feelings and opinions.

The decision to interview the children in groups rather than individually was based, in part, on time constraints. In addition, as I was using a cassette player to record the children's responses, I was particularly concerned to ensure that they felt comfortable and confident enough to talk openly about their views. I did, however, have a number of reservations about undertaking group interviews. I recognised that, as some questions referred specifically to gender, within the group setting the children may have been more preoccupied with defending their self-image as a boy or girl rather than with giving honest responses to my questions. In reality, there were occasions when I sensed that particular boys were choosing to play the 'gender game' – several of the older boys, for example, presented as 'cool' and disinterested while others jeered at some of the girls' responses and what they described as 'girls' stories'. (At this point, I was not able to control my impulse to intervene on behalf of the girls.)

Data analysis

The issue of analysis is a complex one and, as we shall see in Chapter 7, it was the aspect of school-based research with which the teachers had most difficulty. Miles and Huberman (1994) see analysis as consisting of three concurrent flows of activity: data reduction, data display and conclusion drawing/verification. Similarly, Dey (1993) defines it in terms of three related processes: describing, classifying and connecting.

In dealing with data from the first three phases of this research, these 'flows of activity' or 'processes' were apparent, although they were not always easy to disentangle. For example, 'reduction' was ongoing from the start of the research. When interviewing teachers and children, in considering what issues to probe further I was already making decisions about what may be of significance. In addition, as Miles and Huberman (1994) point out, what you see in a transcription is also selective; it is an integral part of simplifying and transforming the written transcriptions and also of making sense of the data. Ely *et al.* comment that we do not find or see meaning in the data, we '*compose* meaning that the data may lead us to understand' (1997: 20).

As an aid to data analysis, I did make use of codes, although the nature of these codes changed as the research progressed. Early on in the research I tended to use descriptive 'first-level' codes (Miles and Huberman 1994) which simply summarised segments of data; for example, 'reading' and 'planning sheets'. As I became more involved in the research, however, I tended to make more use of what Miles and Huberman refer to as 'pattern codes' – smaller analytical units which identify themes and possible causal links. I therefore noted references to, for example, 'power' and 'resistance'.

To suggest that coding formed the basis of my analysis, however, would be to overstate its importance. Rather, codes were heuristic devices for discovery (Seidel and Kelle 1995), providing ways of structuring, interacting with and thinking about the data (Coffey and Atkinson 1996). Like Coffey and Atkinson (1996), therefore, I preferred to think in terms of generating concepts from and with my data, and of seeing coding simply as a means to achieve this end. As analysis proceeded, patterns or themes 'emerged' or, rather, tended to jump into my mind – often when I was not even aware of having been thinking about the data. I was however, mindful of the dangers of this: in each study there was a sense of exhilaration when suddenly I was able to construct a frame that seemed to clarify, order and explain the data. Miles and Huberman (1994) warn that, as patterns just 'happen' – almost too quickly – it is important to see added evidence of the same pattern and to remain open to disconfirming evidence when it appears.

Like Coffey and Atkinson (1996), I found that analysis was not complete after coding or even after the emergence and evaluation of patterns. Coffey and Atkinson argue that writing is important in that it makes us think about our data in new and different ways. They state: 'Thinking about how to represent our data also forces us to think about meanings and understandings, voices and experiences present in the data. As such, writing actually deepens our level of analytic endeavour' (1996: 109).

Writing, to an extent, is a pedagogical strategy. It was through attempting to communicate my findings to an audience (to the teachers with whom I was working and in the writing of this book) that a number of inconsistencies came to light. Often there was an intuitive awareness that some aspect of my argument was in tension with remembered snatches of dialogue or observations. Miles and Huberman (1994) comment that: 'Qualitative analyses can be evocative, illuminating, masterful – and wrong. The story, well told as it is, does not fit the data' (1994: 262).

Although I acknowledged the temptation to come up with a 'neat' explanation, to lop off the many loose ends of which social life is made (Miles and Huberman 1994), I recognised the need to return to the data at this point to test out and re-evaluate my interpretations of emerging patterns and themes. As Coffey and Atkinson point out: 'The emphasis on the "negative" exceptions as well as the "positive" patterns remains crucial' (1996: 47).

In analysing the data, therefore, it appeared that while in one sense I was constrained by the need for rigour and to be systematic in, for example, the testing and retesting of my interpretations and emergent 'meanings', at the same time I recognised the need to be 'endlessly creative and interpretative' (Denzin and Lincoln 1994: 14).

It is important to emphasise that in this project, I recognised the impact of myself as researcher on the collection, analysis and interpretation of data. As with the teachers (and children) with whom I worked, I also brought my implicit theories to this research. Ely *et al.* refer to these theories as 'a set of eyeglasses through which we look at the world' (1997: 228). I recognised that this was an issue, particularly in the first and third phases of the research where I was undertaking the interviews, interpreting the data and feeding the findings back to teachers. I was aware that the 'prejudice' of the researcher cannot be removed from qualitative research. But nor should we attempt to do so (Hammersley and Atkinson 1983): it would be misguided and in any case impossible to try to edit myself out of the text (Gitlin *et al.* 1993).

Validity and reliability

Validity is recognised as an important aspect of data analysis (see, for example, Wolcott 1990, 1994). Although given the nature of the research I was not claiming these findings could be generalised to the whole teacher population, it was necessary to consider the *internal* validity (Schofield 1993) or authenticity (Guba and Lincoln 1994) of data. For example, were teachers interpreting questions in similar ways and were we reaching a shared understanding? And was I interpreting replies as the respondents intended? Moreover, I was aware that those teachers (and children) who were more forthcoming were not necessarily proposing views that were representative.

Mindful of this, in the first study (teachers' perceptions) I made use of respondent validation: feeding back raw data for confirmation (see Ely *et al.* 1991) as well as deliberately testing out alternative explanations. For example, on occasions I asserted a particular view of 'what was going on' and asked the respondent how far this represented his or her understandings. Moreover, after the final analysis, my interpretations of the findings were presented to the teachers for comment and discussion.

Validity was a particular issue in relation to the discussions with children. I was aware that, with the youngest pupils, in particular, when one child gave an answer that was deemed 'reasonable', the others tended to echo this response. In addition, as I have indicated above, there was the issue of how far children's responses reflected the reality of the situation – particularly when they specifically related to gender. For example, if an older boy claimed he *hated* writing in school, was he being truthful or just protecting his 'macho' image?

Ethics

In any research project the issue of ethics is likely to be problematic. Miles and Huberman (1994), for example, identify a series of issues that typically need attention before, during and after qualitative studies. These will incorporate questions such as: do the people I am working with have full information about what the project will involve? Is their consent to participate freely given? What might the project do (inadvertently) to hurt the people involved? Am I telling the truth? Do we trust each other? In what ways will the project 'intrude': come closer to people than they want?

The issue of confidentiality represented an ongoing rather than an intermittent concern (Walker 1993). In all the studies, from the outset, this issue was explored and agreed. There were occasions, both when audio-recording interviews and in group discussions, when teachers maintained that they wanted to say something 'off the record'. However frustrating this was for me as a researcher, I recognised that 'people own the facts of their own lives' (Walker 1993: 192); participants' wishes were therefore respected. Similarly, when interviewing the children there were occasions when, for whatever reason, a child made a negative comment about his or her teacher. This presented me with a dilemma: was it my responsibility to tell the truth, to present the findings as they were or should I protect teachers from comments which I believed they would find upsetting? Ultimately, I decided to use my judgement and, rather than feeding back the detail of the comment, I noted that the children had 'raised this as an issue'.

Conclusion

In this chapter I have outlined the structure of this project and considered a number of research methods and issues. While these methods and issues are contextualised within those aspects of the research with which I had direct involvement, it is hoped that this discussion will also prove useful for teachers wanting to undertake school-based research.

At the beginning of this project, I noted that the approach adopted was initially characterised as 'action research'. In many ways, the project did fit into the action research paradigm: particularly that of 'practical' action research. I commented that the initial phases of the research could be seen as a process of collecting baseline evidence in preparation for the teachers' own explorations. Carr and Kemmis state that 'practical' action research is so labelled because it develops the practical reasoning of practitioners. In this type of research, 'outside facilitators form cooperative relationships with practitioners, helping them to articulate their own concerns, plan strategic action for change, monitor the problems and effects of changes, and reflect on the value and consequences of the changes actually achieved' (Carr and Kemmis 1986: 203).

But Carr and Kemmis emphasise that all those involved in the research process should participate equally in all phases of planning, acting, observing and reflecting. As we have seen, this was not the case in this project. Rather than trying to squeeze the project into the action research paradigm, then, it might be better defined as school-based research involving partnership with outsiders and making use of a variety of research methods.

Earlier in this chapter I also commented that Mortimore (1998), adapting the work of Joyce (1991), refers to the idea of 'doors' which can be opened from the inside in order to support School Improvement. I would argue that as part of this project the teachers did open the doors marked 'research', 'self-evaluation', 'teaching and learning' and 'partnerships'. Moreover, in the following academic year School Improvement was to be sustained through a door opened from the outside: St Thomas was to be involved in a project led by the LEA. As the focus of the new project was to be on improving literacy, teachers were intending to use this as an opportunity to pursue and develop their individual and collaborative explorations.

The idea of 'partnerships', of course, links to my involvement in this research. Although, for me, there was some tension between my dual role as both collaborator and researcher, the teachers commented on what they saw to be the benefits of involvement with an 'outside agency'. The teachers maintained that as I was, in one sense, an 'outsider', I was able to see things with greater clarity – my judgement was not clouded by, for example, their in-depth knowledge of the children. In addition, they maintained that the process of being interviewed, of 'hearing' and reflecting on what they had said in the interview, as well as considering my analysis of the data, had been, 'extremely useful' and had 'certainly made them think'. Moreover, having the involvement of an outsider meant that they felt a sense of urgency and responsibility to get things done: within their busy workload, this research became more of a priority. But, as we shall see in Chapter 7, the fact that this project did not have external funding also meant that there were constraints on the amount of time I could give to this research and this meant that the potential benefits of partnership were not fulfilled. In terms of School Improvement, I would argue that partnership is a powerful tool ... but it also costs!

Part II
Complications

4 Teachers' perceptions of boys, girls and the teaching of literacy[1]

'It's the way they tell them'

At the initial project meeting, the teachers appeared to have clear views about how gender differences related to children's literacy skills. For example, the teachers maintained that they were able to tell whether a piece of writing was by a boy or a girl just by looking at the handwriting and reading the first few sentences. As an initial activity, therefore, it was decided that it would be useful to interview teachers individually in order to ascertain and further explore these perceptions. In terms of literacy skills – and particularly in terms of writing – what exactly did the teachers see as the key differences between boys and girls? What did they believe to be the specific difficulties experienced by boys? And what, therefore, did teachers think of as 'good' writing?

Emerging patterns

It is important to emphasise that, when interviewed, all the teachers stressed that they were making generalised statements; they maintained that there would always be individuals who did not conform to the stereotypes they were describing. However, even in the reception classes, differences between boys and girls' behaviour were noted. For example, Jacqui explained that:

> when it comes to constructional activities the boys are very much more involved in constructing cars and building and they are very much more active in the classroom across the board. They'll get involved in some role-play activity which wouldn't necessarily mean sitting down in the home corner drinking tea – they're running around the classroom because one's a policeman and one's a crook – and they use the whole room ... whereas girls tend to sit more.

Jacqui also commented that 'boys have to be encouraged, continually encouraged' and that whereas the girls tended to engage in more extended play, 'boys have a shorter attention span and then they're off to play with something else'.

In addition, even at this early stage, there was a perceived difference in attitudes towards reading and writing. Jacqui maintained that while both boys and girls enjoyed listening to stories, it was girls who were more likely to be seen sitting quietly and reading a book. Jacqui and Melanie agreed that the girls in their classes appeared to enjoy writing activities more than the boys did. Jacqui commented:

> If I ask them to come and undertake a writing activity ... apart from one or two it's mostly the girls who would ask to undertake it whereas the boys, you would have to ask them ... the girls seem to enjoy writing. From an early age they seem to enjoy it.

Moreover, it was noted that boys and girls tended to use the writing corner for different purposes. Jacqui commented that whereas girls tended to make lists and write invitations, if the corner was set up as a post office, for example, boys were much more likely to 'stamp over things rather than to actually make writing and make marks'.

Boys and girls of this age were also seen as having different reading preferences and to approach texts in different ways. For example, Melanie commented: 'they [boys] like to remember the long names [of dinosaurs], to remember facts ... they like pictures of blood dripping and things like that'.

In addition, Melanie maintained that when talking about ideas for their stories, the older reception class boys were 'streets ahead' of the girls: this was because 'they've already got a creative spark'. Moreover, Melanie reflected that whereas boys' stories tended to include 'fierce, fantastic language', girls' stories, while more detailed, were often 'trite'.

In Years 1–6, these emerging attitudes and behaviours appeared to become more marked. For example, boys were perceived to prefer listening to and reading stories about sport and, in particular, about horror and ghosts; in fact, as Gaynor commented, 'anything with a bit of blood and thunder in it'.

Gareth commented that in his experience boys also showed a particular interest in more factual texts. For example, he stated that: 'Boys very often like information books so they can ... find things out about a particular subject. It could be scientific, sporting ... about the world around them. And generally, girls enjoy reading fiction more than boys.' Similarly, Gaynor commented: 'Boys tend to go for the facts. Thinking back to last year's class it's been a case of ... "Look what I've found out".'

Glenda maintained that she felt non-fiction appealed to boys as it did not require the stamina and perseverance that was needed to read fiction – rather, 'they can just dip into it'. That said, Glenda felt that the girls in her class were equally interested in non-fiction but chose to find out about different topics from the boys. Reflecting on a recent activity, she maintained: 'the girls were going for things like pets and the boys were going for mini-beasts, creepy-crawlies. One picked a book on horses, another armour.'

The teachers maintained that boys' reluctance to read was particularly apparent during 'silent reading' time: the 20 minutes at the beginning of the day when children were expected to choose a book and read quietly to themselves. Amanda commented: 'When I see the children in the class-room, especially during "silent reading" time, the boys just don't want to read ... they hate reading. The children who are negative about reading ... a high percentage of them are boys.'

The teachers maintained that boys' negative attitudes to reading were often commented on by parents. Simon noted, for example, that 'On several occasions I've had parents of boys saying ... he's not like his sister, he never goes to his bedroom to read.'

The problem with stories

Writing stories:[2] attitudes and ability

One pattern of behaviour commented on by all the teachers was boys' reluctance to write. For example, Glenda commented: 'In science lessons the interest would be there across the board for practical work, but as soon as the science sheet had to be written up the girls carried on and the boys ... the attitude ... '

This reluctance was particularly noticeable when the children were asked to write a story and, despite the teachers' commitment to providing a range of writing, it was agreed that there tended to be, in Amanda's words, 'a heavy focus on creative writing'. This was particularly the case lower down in the school where story writing was seen as 'traditional': as Amanda commented 'children don't start with non-fiction writing – they tell stories about their lives'. Teachers stressed that the overwhelming diffi-culty in this respect was not boys' ability but their attitude; Glenda commented: 'I've had some very bright boys who liked writing. But there are also some boys who are not so bright that liked writing. I can't say it always relates to ability.'

More often, however, teachers commented on those boys who appeared 'able' – particularly in suggesting ideas for stories – but who were extremely reluctant to record their ideas on paper. Teachers maintained that in whole-class discussion 'on the carpet', it was boys who dominated the discussion. Girls, it was stated, would tend to 'sit quietly and listen' whereas the boys were 'really keen, hands up all over the place'. In addi-tion, it was the boys who 'suggested interesting ideas' and demonstrated 'sensitive use of language'. Emma commented, for example:

> On the carpet the boys are very keen and completely dominant ... the
> girls are quieter. The boys are always very keen to listen to stories and

their feedback ... their ideas are fantastic ... Their choice of descriptions and ... they choose more elaborate words when describing ... like a dragon ... a *ferocious* dragon ... The boys this year come up with some lovely ideas ... the glistening rain, the rain dancing on his hat ... I don't know where they get it from.

But discussing ideas for stories appeared to be a different issue from recording these ideas on paper. As Paula explained, 'The children go to their tables and between the carpet and the table something mysterious happens to them and suddenly ... they start off quite keen and then it's a chore and it's too much like hard work ... '

Several teachers maintained that for many boys, regardless of ability, the main concern was 'How much have I got to write?' Emma maintained:

> In terms of writing, I think I've got four or five girls who find it difficult, that's because they can't write independently ... while the rest of the girls can sit down, finish a piece of work, not need much assistance really. Boys, I've got nearer ten boys, four or five who find writing a real struggle, possibly another five who do not actually enjoy writing ... there's a bigger proportion of boys that are lazier, basically.

In addition, teachers referred to boys' problem with concentration and maintained that they were easily distracted. For example, Emma noted that 'they're always sharpening their pencils' and that 'they start off with one or two lines and then ... The girls stay on task better.'

While many teachers stressed that a negative attitude towards writing stories applied to the majority of boys, it was particularly acute in those described as of 'lower ability': Gareth commented that getting written work from these Year 6 boys was 'like getting blood from a stone'. It was not only coming up with ideas that these boys found difficult but also handwriting, spelling and punctuation. Other teachers also commented:

> The less able boys they just hate writing, they find it such a chore. They know they're not going to be able to spell things, they can't be bothered with the detail, punctuation and so on ... They find it hard to settle to writing ... they find it hard to pursue something to the end. Even handwriting – if they've got a lot to write, the handwriting deteriorates and then they're not proud of their work and lose interest in it ...
>
> (Christine)

> I think the strugglers find it hard ... it's such an effort for them to write a story. With a story, if they're only capable of writing four lines, it's very difficult to make a story that you can read back to the class.
>
> (Emma)

In story writing I find that band of poor children ... the ones that are not so able ... they flick from one tense to another, they find it hard to stay in the past tense if they're writing. And instead of saying 'were' they say 'was' – that kind of thing.

(Amanda)

Indeed, in all but the high ability group untidy handwriting and poor spelling were described as 'typical' features of boys' writing. Unsurprisingly, then, motivating boys to write was highlighted as a particular problem. Teachers maintained that for girls the motivation was, essentially, to please the teacher: 'to make the teacher happy and to do what they think you want' (Paula). But this was not believed to be the case with boys. Paula explained:

I think boys are motivated by different things. Competition is a huge thing for boys, being better than somebody else ... but pleasing you isn't an issue for boys, they're not bothered by what *you* really want. They'll do it if they get a star ... there's got to be something else ... like using the computer.

Similarly, Gareth commented:

Girls want to please I find ... The ability might not be that much better but they want to put something down for you and make the teacher happy. A lot of the boys couldn't care less ... I think boys have to be stimulated more ... it's got to be something exciting, or something sporty. You've got to put more input to get something out ... you've got to encourage them ... stimulate them.

Paula noted that this competitive attitude did not only apply to writing. She also commented that the boys:

were really keen on the reading scheme ... because J's on the red books and S's on the green books ... and as soon as they come off the scheme a lot of them think ... that's it now. They stop bringing their readers in, their mums say they're not reading much at home. And I was thinking, the competition thing again ...

The consequence of boys' attitude in this respect was to place real demands on teachers' time and patience. Teachers maintained that these demands were particularly noticeable when boys were asked to write stories and, unsurprisingly, several teachers noted that this was a form of writing they liked to teach least. As Emma maintained: 'I find story writing very hard ... with a class of 32 it's very hard ... and with the strugglers ... ' Similarly Paula noted: 'I think story writing is one of the most difficult things to teach ... I've got to be in a really good mood to do story because it's a lot of work, a lot of input.' Simon also commented that story writing was 'one of the tougher types of lessons to do'.

Language issues

A further difficulty referred to by the teachers related specifically to boys' use of language. That is, in their story writing boys were often reluctant to incorporate descriptive or figurative language: what several teachers referred to as 'flowery' language. Several teachers suggested that boys might perceive this type of language as being gendered: 'girlie writing'. Glenda commented:

> I think the boys feel less comfortable using expressive language, which is the sort of language I am trying to get them to use ... I think it's because it's considered girlish. The girls will sit and write reams about the wonderful sky and the scene and talk about this, that and the other whereas the boys will ... 'I don't want to get involved in all that.'

In addition, teachers maintained that boys' stories often lacked detail: boys didn't take the time to set the scene or talk about characters but wanted to get 'straight into the action'. Simon explained:

> At the start of the term we talked in quite a lot of depth about intro-duction to stories – setting the scene, talking about characters, using description. And I found that a lot of those ideas weren't really taken on board by a lot of the boys – they wanted to get into the action part of it ... quite a lot of dialogue ... which wasn't really punctuated prop-erly ... quite a lot of their friends involved. And really moving away from the things I wanted them to include. They were keener, not really to set the scene but to get involved in the action part of it, tell about their friends who were involved, the fights and whatever.

Moreover, while girls were willing to write a story based on a title given by the teacher, this was not the case with the boys. Amanda commented:

> Given a choice of three stories girls will be happy to choose one of those and write about it ... There is uproar with the boys when I give them the choice of three. They want to write their own story ... an idea that they have in their head.

Writing in other language forms

But while the boys had difficulties with writing stories, the teachers all commented on their enthusiasm for writing poetry and their ability to 'achieve good results' in this language form. Teachers suggested a number of reasons why this may have been the case. For example, Paula stated:

> I think the sheer length of a story is a big thing ... with poetry they can get their ideas down quickly in a succinct way and don't have to worry whether it's got a beginning, a middle and an end ... and they don't have to write in sentences ...

Moreover, teachers stated that when writing poetry, boys did appear willing to use descriptive or figurative language – linguistic devices such as metaphor and simile – and also to focus on the affective. Glenda commented, for example, that 'in terms of that expressive side, I don't find the same reluctance with poetry writing'. Simon suggested that it was possibly the narrower and defined focus and the tighter and more obvious structure of the poem that encouraged the boys to be more descriptive.

Not only did boys prefer writing poetry to writing stories but, teachers maintained, they generally preferred writing in non-narrative to narrative language forms. That is, while boys' difficulties were not purely located in story writing, 'in these other forms they can achieve' (Emma). Teachers again attributed this to the quantity of the writing involved: for example, 'some of the boys prefer that style because ... they can put some ideas down ... and it's not pages and pages' (Simon).

However, several teachers also referred to boys' difficulties with some non-narrative forms. For example, teachers referred to boys' reluctance to make a written record of practical work – Simon commented on one boy who, when asked to write an account of his scientific experiments, always complained: 'Why do I have to write it down? ... There's no need ... I know it.' Problems highlighted by Christine included:

> not being aware of the reader, not being aware of what the reader knew or didn't know, not giving reasons for things, not realising that you have to have a 'because' in somewhere, and not being able to give the difference between fact and opinion ... working out what to say precisely ... it's all those things.

While girls also had difficulties in this respect, it was felt that they were more likely to 'take on board' what they had been taught; boys, on the other hand, tended to 'go their own way'. For example, it was noted that in writing about a scientific investigation boys did not make use of the conventions of this form but generally wrote the report 'as a story'. Simon commented that the boys would write: 'We did this, we played that and then ... Gary hit me on the head with it ... And nothing focused on the actual science writing.'

Despite their difficulties with story writing, therefore, it appeared that boys were generally more familiar or comfortable with this genre.

'Good' writing

Of course, not all boys had problems with writing; teachers maintained that there were boys who were willing and able to write well. 'Good' writing by boys was generally described as more 'creative', 'exciting', 'alive' and 'imaginative' than writing produced by the girls. Gaynor compared the comments of a Year 1 boy and a girl. The boy asked to produce a caption for a picture of a pirate with a hat over his eyes 'came up with "Oh dear, who's put the lights out", you know, which is different. I'm wondering what the girl has come up with ... "Oh, I can't see" or "Please take the hat off".'

Boys, teachers maintained, were much more likely to use suspense and build up tension in their stories, and also to use the kind of dialogue found in cartoons, videos and computer games; as Simon commented, 'to use things like "Yikes" with lots of big exclamation marks'. Again, teachers indicated that it was 'the way boys told them' that made these boys' stories interesting and better than those produced by the majority of the girls. Teachers commented, for example:

> The good boys ... the breadth of their vocabulary is very good, the structure of their writing is very good ... I would predict that they would produce the best writing in the class.
>
> (Simon)

> Boys are much more creative and they'll go into a different world. And they'll exaggerate things, they'll make things exciting, they'll put interesting things in their stories and write in a descriptive way and make things so much more lively. It's the ideas they string together and the way they use language.
>
> (Amanda)

> Imaginative ... use of really interesting language ... not and then I went de dah de dah de dah. It's usually aliens or ghost stories. Punctuation goes by the bye and so does the spelling ... it's not that ... it's the ideas, the imagination. The girls tend to play safe and the boys will take risks and they'll think of something different, or a different angle. And they'll put speech in it or ... it's more alive.
>
> (Paula)

> They're using a wide vocabulary, they're expressing themselves clearly, their stories are well structured, imaginative ... Boys tend to be more adventurous, they write more dramatic stories, they use more exciting language ... they use a greater range of adjectives, adverbs, complex sentences ... compared with the girls.
>
> (Christine)

Girls' difficulties

As I have indicated above, it was not that girls were necessarily seen by teachers as 'good' speakers and writers – far from it. Girls *were* perceived to enjoy reading and writing more – both in school and out of school. In addition, in their story writing, teachers noted that 'there is more attention to detail and description' (Simon). Moreover, Simon maintained that: 'Girls are more careful with things like punctuation. They will read back their work to check for things ... rather than get it finished.'

However, as we have seen, girls were described as being passive when working 'on the carpet': as listening rather than suggesting ideas. In addition, when given a topic on which to write, girls were less likely to question or object to the teacher's choice. Amanda commented, for example: 'Girls will do as they're told, they're very compliant' and 'The girls just seem to get on with it. They don't seem to question it.'

Glenda similarly maintained 'I'm not sure that the girls are so enthusiastic and the boys are so negative, it's just that the girls accept it ... and the boys don't mind voicing a lack of interest.'

But girls' desire to 'play it safe' was also reflected in the quality of their writing. I noted earlier that Melanie referred to girls' stories as 'trite'. This perception was shared by both Key Stage 1 and Key Stage 2 teachers. For example, Simon stated that girls' stories 'tend to be more predictable on the whole', while Amanda maintained 'The girls tend to be really bland ... they'll write about the mundane.'

However, given the demands of motivating and supporting the boys with their writing, as girls tended 'to just get on and finish their work with much less assistance', it was unsurprising that teachers allowed them to do just that; teachers acknowledged that, even though they were unimpressed with girls' writing, they were more likely to accept it without challenge. Several teachers voiced their concerns that they were 'being tough' on the boys and that they recognised that they expected more of them. Paula maintained:

> I think I'm a little harder on the boys in a way. Well, I've got quite a lot of lively boys, so I've had to be quite tough ... In a way, if the girls do enough, but they've been quite good, they've been quiet and got on with it ... perhaps I wouldn't say to the girls, 'No, come on, get a bit more excitement in there', 'You could get more imagination in there' ... But perhaps I'm a bit tougher on the boys ... expect them to do more.

Discussion and conclusions

In relation to literacy skills, what, then, did the teachers see as the key differences between boys and girls? The teachers maintained that, in their view, gender differences were apparent not only in boys' and girls' use of language, transcription skills, and reading and writing preferences, but also in their attitudes and behaviour. These differences were believed to become more apparent, and to have a greater impact on children's attainment, as they progressed through the school. Moreover, the list of boys' perceived difficulties was long: compared with girls boys needed more encouragement, were less attentive and compliant, were more easily distracted and less likely to complete their work (particularly story writing). In addition, boys were more likely than girls to have problems with spelling and handwriting, while their stories often lacked detail and focused on action at the expense of description.

One further problem identified by the teachers was that, when writing stories, the boys shied away from using figurative and descriptive language; teachers decided that this was because boys considered this to be 'girlie' or gender-marked. However, the teachers also commented that, when writing poetry, the boys did not seem to demonstrate any reluctance to use such language, nor were they afraid to focus on the affective.

In the discussion following the feedback of my findings, the teachers speculated that it was not 'sensitive language use' *per se* that was the problem. Rather, boys' difficulties might be related instead to the (perceived) demands of story writing: for example, the importance of quantity, and the requirement to take into account the multitude of demands – characters, plot, structure, as well as spelling, punctuation and the like. Conversely, the approach they adopted to teaching poetry writing – such as a narrower focus and the use of structure – might enable boys to concentrate on their use of language in order to explore, interpret and express their ideas and feelings.

'Good' writing?

The issue of sensitive or gender-marked language use led to a further consideration by the teachers: what counts as 'good' writing in school? Jackson (Jackson, P. 1998: 2–3), for example, suggests that there is a danger of encouraging children to perceive 'good' narrative writing as that which is 'stuffed full of adjectives and adverbs'. In addition, I noted in Chapter 2 that girls' practices and preferences might be more in keeping with what is understood to be 'legitimate' literacy in school. Alloway and Gilbert (1997) point out that many of the most familiar literacy practices require pupils to 'lay bare the soul' (1997: 55). Is this reasonable, they ask, when outside school boys are encouraged to understand themselves very differently: to concentrate on things outside the self rather than on the self? What is so wrong with the inclusion of ideas gained from the visual medium of television and computer games? According to Millard (1997), methods absorbed from these and other media may be used to convey action – a key theme in boys' writing. Should we take more account of boys' popular cultural interests when planning children's literacy work (see Marsh 1999, 2000a, 2000b; Millard 1997)? And are we clear *why* the development of narrative through dialogue and passages of description is considered preferable to a more episodic, visual narrative style (see Nilan 1995)?

Boys on top?

Despite the long list of difficulties associated with boys' writing, it was noted that in some significant ways boys were described by the teachers as being 'better' than girls were. For example, the teachers maintained that boys were more imaginative and creative and had more interesting ideas. These comments appear to resonate with the ideas of Cohen (1998) who, as I noted in Chapter 1, maintains that, despite poor attainment, boys are often seen as having innate if untapped potential. While girls' successes are attributed to hard work, boys' failures are attributed to something external to them.

Other researchers have made a similar point. Warrington and Younger (2000), for example, note that in their interviews with secondary school teachers it was often apparent that, despite the fact that they praised girls for their conscientious approach to work, they actually preferred to teach boys, who were regarded as more interesting. Warrington and Younger state that, despite girls' achievements, teachers thought that boys were 'livelier in discussion, more willing to voice opinions than girls, and sharper on the uptake' (2000: 504). Warrington and Younger maintain that, among the teachers, there appeared to be almost a concealed admiration for these boys who were described as having a bit of 'sparkle and challenge' as opposed to the more 'middle of the road' girls. Why is this the case? Do female teachers identify with the girls and admire the (masculine) qualities of boys they see as so different from their own?

Despite (or because of) these discussions, the teachers also raised concerns about their attitudes towards and expectations of girls. Several (female) teachers commented that they now felt that it was not right that they accepted girls' passivity simply because it supported the effective management of classes. This was particularly unfair, they claimed, given that they then criticised the impact of this passivity on girls' behaviour and literacy skills. Emma asked, for example: 'Shouldn't girls be encouraged to question and to voice their ideas during class discussions? If their writing is perceived to be boring, shouldn't we explicitly challenge girls in order to develop their skills as well?'

Some of the teachers also expressed their concerns about the possible implications of choosing subject matter that appealed to boys and focusing their language work on non-fiction texts. Glenda, for example, maintained that: 'My big concern is that we're going to swing the balance too far – that the girls are going to be switched off ... '

But this was an early stage of our explorations. Having considered and re-considered teachers' perceptions of the differences and difficulties experienced by boys and girls in relation to the teaching and learning of literacy, it was now felt necessary to move on to the next step: to examine their actual differences and difficulties. This, then, was the next phase of our project and is the focus of Chapter 5.

5   Taking a closer look

Having examined teachers' perceptions of gender differences in relation to the teaching and learning of literacy, as well as the particular difficulties teachers believed were experienced by boys, it was felt necessary to ascertain children's 'actual' differences and difficulties. The teachers therefore identified a sample of six children in each class and over a period of six weeks all writing undertaken by these children was collected and analysed. The first part of this chapter describes and comments on the data collection and on the analysis of this data by the head teacher and teachers: how they approached this, the difficulties they encountered and what they found out. The remainder of the chapter is concerned with my analysis of the children's narrative writing and how far this conforms to the gender differences identified in Chapter 2.

Data collection

The first issue to be addressed was: what data should be collected and from whom? The teachers decided that it was not feasible for them to examine all the writing produced by every child in the school; they would need to collect and analyse writing from a sample group. In addition, if they were to make judgements about the differences between boys' and girls' writing then, within this sample group, they would need to include a cross-section of ability. Teachers eventually decided that within each class they would identify six children – a boy and girl of high, average and low ability – whose writing would be collected over a six-week period. This writing was to be logged in a large lever-arch file: these became known as their project files.

A further issue discussed was how to organise the data in order to aid analysis. A pro forma was eventually devised which included the following headings:

- date of activity;
- lead person (teacher/student/supply teacher);
- writing category;

- context for activity (brief points only, e.g. main aims, inputs, audience etc.);
- any other significant comments (e.g. outcomes, children's comments).

For each writing activity, teachers completed one pro forma and this was attached to the samples of the children's work.

Difficulties

When it came to analysing the writing the teachers recognised that there were difficulties with the data collection. First, some of the classes had student teachers on block teaching placements and these students had been involved in the planning and teaching of the literacy work – this obviously affected the 'normal' balance of pupil activities. In addition, while some students had been careful to complete the pro forma and log the sample children's work in the file, others had not been so reliable. This difficulty was not helped by the fact that many of the writing samples had been photocopied from children's books. This meant that some pieces of writing were incomplete or difficult to read. Moreover, pupil absences also contributed to work missing from the teachers' files.

A further difficulty related to the choice of children in the sample group. At a project meeting the teachers acknowledged that classifying the children as having average, below average or above average language skills had been problematic. Some teachers expressed surprise about children in other classes who had been categorised as of 'high' or 'low' ability. This discussion revealed a confusion over whether individual children should be judged in relation to teachers' generalised knowledge of what was deemed to be of 'average' ability for a boy or a girl, or 'average' ability in relation to the particular class of children they were teaching this year. The teachers maintained that, in general, while there were a few 'very good' boys, there were many more girls than boys who fell into the 'average' or 'above average' band of ability and many more boys than girls whom they would describe as 'below average'. In many cases, therefore, the collection of children's work, revealed that a 'below average' girl was often working at a similar level to an 'average' boy.

Beginning the analysis

Despite these difficulties, the work contained in the teachers' files provided an enormous amount of valuable evidence. As a way of 'getting into' this data, Dave, the head teacher, asked the teachers to analyse the different types of writing tasks undertaken by the children. As an aid to this analysis, the teachers used eleven categories that were suggested by the LEA English Adviser. However, even with this support, the teachers found that categorising the children's work in this way was not an easy task, and some teachers appeared reluctant to place particular activities into a specific category, or were unsure about which category to use. Once this task had been completed, however, at a subsequent staff meeting the teachers' responses were presented to them in the form of tables:

Table 1 Reception/Key Stage 1 teachers' assignments of children's work

	Jacqui	*Melanie*	*Gaynor*	*Emma*
Narrative		8	8	5
Report	3	1	1	1
Argument				
Persuasion				
Poem	1	4	2	2
Instruction		1	1	1
Explanation		3		
Play script				
Letter	1	1	3	3
Journal	1		6	6
Non-specific	1		1	1

Table 2 Key Stage 2 teachers' assignments of children's work

	Paula	*Glenda*	*Simon*	*Amanda*	*Christine*
Narrative	2	6	2	5	4
Report	2	1	2	4	2
Argument			1	1	1
Persuasion			1	4	3
Poem	2	3	1	3	1
Instruction	1	2			
Explanation		3	4	4	4
Play script	1				2
Letter	1				1
Journal		5			2
Non-specific	8		1	2	2

A consideration of Tables 1 and 2 enabled teachers to share their concerns and difficulties about categorisation. They also discussed how the work undertaken during the six-week period related to the range of writing activities undertaken over the whole year. This led to further debate about whether certain forms of writing were more appropriate to particular stages of children's literacy development or whether children of all ages should experience the full range of writing forms. In addition, teachers expressed their concerns that, as yet, they were not mapping out children's literacy experiences across different classes and key stages in any detail. What were the expectations, for example, of children's narrative writing in Year 4, compared with Year 5 and Year 6? What was the progression between children in each year group?

At this meeting the teachers also examined each other's project files and made an initial comparison of the quality and quantity of the children's work. It was noted that in their discussions the teachers tended to home in on the 'specifics' of individual children – their central focus was the individual child and his or her achievements – for example, 'Look how R has improved' or 'Isn't that typical of M?'

The teachers also commented on the different ways in which the pro forma had been completed. It was apparent that comments on the pro forma varied – some teachers wrote just enough information to remind themselves about the context of the activity or to note absent children while others used the pro forma to comment on individual children or to record their thoughts and ideas. For example:

> Children were to report back on points taken from old photographs of Swansea beach. They were to recall as many points as possible. The children were able to discuss the points but found it difficult to put their ideas down. Writing factually and not about themselves made the task extremely difficult.
>
> (Melanie)

> Having made a key for our own maps of St Thomas I wanted children to be able to use the key to discover information from the map. We looked at the map first and read through the key – looked at how they were related. We read through questions as a class and talked about how we would locate information. I emphasised that only brief answers were needed and not full sentences. The majority of children coped well with this. The boys really seemed enthusiastic and interested. Again, there weren't massive amounts of text to wade through. The skill was knowing how to locate the information.
>
> I think the fact that it was relevant – it had actually taken place – helped a lot. R (girl) particularly struggled with this piece of work and was helped by a more able child to complete work. I think the format of the activity completely threw her! The less able boys coped with this, however.
>
> (Paula)

> M (boy) found it difficult to write about made-up characters – he wanted to write about himself. He required a considerable amount of teacher input with regard to ideas. He seemed to forget about writing

in sentences as his story progressed. M failed to finish his story – he was unable to pace himself – although he was given sufficient time.

(Gareth)

The impact of teachers on gender identity

One issue raised by Dave at this meeting was how far teachers' written responses to the children's work might impact on the children's developing gender identity. This was particularly the case with the early years/Key Stage 1 teachers who were often less subject-specific in their comments, and who were more inclined to instigate a dialogue with the children. Dave noted that responses to girls' stories tended to emphasise the sad/gentle/compassionate side of their natures – 'Did you hurt yourself, Lucy?' – while responses to the boys' stories were more likely to focus on the action – 'Was daddy speeding?'. Dave wondered whether teachers might also unwittingly stifle girls' daring through feigning shock or horror in response to girls' accounts of minor misdemeanours. As an example, Dave noted the seeming 'acceptance' of several incidents of bad behaviour included in the recount of one boy, whereas a girl in the same class who admitted that she had accidentally broken a window with a stone had provoked the comment 'Oh no, Sian!'

Following this meeting, the teachers were asked to spend some time re-reading, considering and discussing the data and to make written comments on their findings. Below is a summary of some of the points made.

Reception and Year 1

In terms of their attitudes towards writing, Gaynor felt that there was little difference between boys and girls although Jacqui and Melanie noted that the boys appeared to be less inclined than the girls were to persevere with writing activities. All three teachers agreed, however, that from their evaluation of the data there appeared to be no apparent gender differences in the early development of writing skills such as handwriting and spelling.

Jacqui, Melanie and Gaynor noted that, with the youngest children, one of the most significant factors in the quantity of writing produced was the extent to which children had developed fine motor skills. This, they main-tained, was particularly evident when the children were asked to undertake a more challenging writing task, such as writing a story. The teachers also noted that the quality of the boys' written work was greatly improved when there was careful consideration of the initial stimulus, when the subject-matter appealed to boys' interests and when the work was care-fully structured – for example, when the writing task was broken down into short sentences.

Years 2–4

Emma, Paula and Glenda also commented on children's difficulties with longer, sustained pieces of writing such as story writing. For the boys, this was attributed to their lack of concentration and perseverance in relation to the demands of story writing. Emma wrote, for example:

> In my class this year boys appear to have poorer concentration spans than many of the girls. This particularly affects their written work which requires a greater amount of sustained effort than other activities, for example, number work, where it is often a case of solving one problem then another. With writing this may not always be the case and work can therefore become disjointed. This is where writing lists, instructions, rules, etc. becomes easier as the very nature of the writing is in point form. Story writing requires connecting sentences, a flow of ideas and a sensible sequence of events.

Not only did the girls demonstrate greater concentration and perseverance than the boys, they were also seen to be more responsive to advice and were motivated to 'get it right'. Glenda maintained, for example, that: 'The girls in the sample group like to see a nicely presented piece of writing and spend time improving their handwriting.'

Like the teachers of the youngest children, Paula and Emma also commented on the significance of structure. Paula, for example, maintained that the less structure or scaffolding offered, the more difficult it was to gain quality writing from children.

Years 5–6

Amanda and Christine reported that they had become acutely aware that many of the children found it very difficult to express themselves clearly, precisely and accurately in writing. Amanda commented that, when undertaking a reading comprehension task, for example, the children's answers were often very brief and not always appropriate. Some children, she noted, did not distinguish between 'how' and 'why' questions. Moreover, when writing an argument or a piece of writing that required them to 'compare and contrast', the children did not always have the correct vocabulary in order to articulate their ideas, nor the skills needed to organise these ideas effectively. While recognising that speech and writing are different processes with different structures in terms of grammar and syntax, Christine 'felt sure' that there *was* a link with the difficulties many of the children demonstrated in their spoken language. She asked: 'Should we be concentrating earlier on clear spoken communication so that grammatical structures are more ingrained?'

In addition, the Year 5–6 teachers commented on boys' reluctance to spend time planning their writing. Amanda noted, for example, that: 'Boys are not eager to think through their work and plan it. They tend to launch into tasks and see the planning side as a waste of time. They'll say: "I *know* what I want to say." '

The teachers maintained that this reluctance to plan meant that the stories, particularly of the less able boys, often lacked direction and characterisation. Christine noted that these boys often began well but failed to finish their stories satisfactorily.

Similar gender differences were noted in relation to the redrafting of work. Amanda commented that 'boys find re-reading work a chore and do not take this seriously'. She maintained that although this may also be the case with girls, they tended to be more compliant or less obvious in their resistance. She cited one boy who, when asked to redraft his work, said 'What's the point?' Moreover, these teachers maintained that, while difficulties with, for example, spelling and punctuation were found in the work of both boys and girls, these difficulties were more visible or acute in the writing of the boys.

Amanda noted that the boys, in particular, often complained that they found the actual writing process physically tiring. It may be of significance, she suggested, that the boys tended to be more precise in their writing when the task was shorter or more structured. Amanda recognised that this was also true for girls but, she maintained, whereas the girls usually motivated themselves to see a task through to the end, the boys needed 'real encouragement'. Simon similarly commented that when they got into difficulties with their writing the boys appeared to lack the perseverance to overcome these difficulties and to complete the task. Christine suggested that it was this greater perseverance that had enabled some girls to achieve higher than expected SATs results.

But although girls' demonstrated more positive attitudes towards writing, showed greater concentration and perseverance, and were often neater and more accurate in their spelling and punctuation, the teachers maintained that in terms of the composition, boys' stories were often 'better' than those written by the girls. Christine referred to the stories of the 'weaker' girls which, she maintained, tended to focus on immediate friends and the local environment. Amanda similarly commented (as the teachers had done in the initial interviews) that girls' stories tended to be 'bland' and that boys have more creative ideas. In addition, she stated that boys were more adventurous with their vocabulary. Even though this presented difficulties with spelling, she felt that boys were more willing to accept mistakes in their work whereas girls were less prepared to take risks for fear of getting it wrong.

Summary

What, then did the teachers conclude from this analysis? Overall, the teachers maintained that their perceptions about the differences between the attitudes and writing of boys and girls had been correct. However, this exploration had revealed that gender differences were much less obvious than they had anticipated. For example, teachers maintained that while girls were, in general, neater than boys were, this was not always the case; they had noticed many examples of girls' work that were also untidy. Significantly, the teachers argued that there appeared to be a greater correlation between children's difficulties with spelling, punctuation and handwriting and their general ability with language work rather than their gender. But teachers' comments about the nature of these gender differences warrant a closer inspection.

Composition and transcription

It has been suggested (Smith 1982) that the writing process can be subdivided into two broad but interlinking aspects: composition and transcription. Composition includes ideas, vocabulary and grammar while transcription includes the physical effort of writing, spelling, punctuation[1] and handwriting. Although the popularity and appeal of the process approach has been superseded by the genre-based approach to the teaching of writing (see Chapter 8), this distinction, while rather simplistic, is useful for examining the teachers' comments.

In looking at children's writing, the teachers appeared to accept the view of Barrs (1987) that the emphasis, first and foremost, should be on composition rather than transcription. The teachers also implied that whereas most aspects of transcription could be taught, the essence of composition – coming up with good ideas – could not. I noted in Chapter 1 that Cohen (1998) argues that despite their poor attainment in tests and examinations, boys are often seen as having innate potential while girls' successes are often dismissed as simply being the result of hard work. In Chapter 4 I related this to the teachers' comments that, despite citing a long list of boys' difficulties with literacy, in some significant ways they perceived the boys to be 'better' than the girls: for example, they saw them as being more creative and imaginative.

In this study, having reviewed the children's writing, the teachers indicated that it was transcription skills – those aspects of writing which are essentially 'taught' – that were the most positive feature of girls' writing. However, these difficulties with transcription skills they saw as not related to gender but to children's 'general ability' in writing. Composition, on the other hand – 'what powers the writing' (Barrs 1987: 2) – was seen by the teachers as more to do with innate ability. Moreover, this was the aspect of writing at which the 'best' boys excelled. Thus, in line with Cohen (1998), girls' strengths in writing were seen as being related to hard work, while boys' strengths were related to their 'natural' ability. In addition, teachers indicated that children's (boys' and girls') difficulties with transcription could be improved through teaching. Difficulties with important aspects of composition, however, could not.

My explorations

Following this meeting I borrowed the teachers' files in order to examine the samples of writing for myself. I focused on the children's narratives – specifically the younger children's recounts and the older children's stories. In examining these narratives, I was not intending to make judgements on their worth as stories. Nor was I interested in issues such as handwriting, spelling and punctuation. Rather, I wanted to explore how far children's gender identities were demonstrated in these narratives.

Reception and Key Stage 1

In the reception and Key Stage 1 classes, most of the writing undertaken during this six-week period had been based around the picture books the children studied as part of their language work; there were few examples of narratives which related to the events and challenges of their daily lives. Where children did write their own stories, these powerfully reflected their understanding and demonstration of gender roles. In the following short narrative by a Year 1 boy, for example, he manages to include references to pursuits associated with the stereotypical 'macho man': swearing, fighting and drinking.

> I wacht Jeery Pring (Jerry Springer) show there was lodes of fitting and lodes of sweirig there but my nan let's me watch it ven I fell a sleep
>
> And ven I had a nihtmer (nightmare) and then the next day I went to sea Anastasea the bit I liket was all of it I was tiad ven I went home and ven the next day I went back over my nanas and did nothing
>
> I went to a crissnine (christening) after the crissnine I went to the pub there were lots of people I was having a bad sumuake (stomach) ven i had a dringk and I had 20 dringks to carme me down ven we had food and it was over it was much better.

However, examples of personal narratives were few and as my main interest was in exploring gender awareness I focused on the work – the stories – of the Key Stage 2 classes. Sixty stories by children from five Key Stage 2 classes were examined – that is, all the narratives included in these teachers' files that were complete and legible. Of these 60 stories, 37 were written by boys and the remaining 23 by girls.

As I noted in Chapter 2, from the literature it appears that girls' writing is more likely to be set in the home and involve domestic or family themes. Girls, it is suggested, are also more likely to write in the tradition of fairy stories, while older girls tend to write about love and romance. Boys, on the other hand, write about superheroes and bad guys, their stories often being fantasies of power and domination. Boys' stories tend to involve assertive central characters and are written in the first person – girls, being both the observers and the observed, are more likely to write in the third person. When girls do include heroes in their stories these are not self-sufficient but tend to be dependent on others for help and companionship. Boys' stories are action-packed, often making use of the language of comics or cartoons and, unlike the stories of girls, there is little use of dialogue, detail or description, nor reference to emotion or relationships. But were these differences easily apparent in the narratives written by the children in the sample group?

Happy ever after?

Few of the stories I examined focused directly on domestic or family themes, although children – both boys and girls – often ended their adventures by going or returning home. In addition, there were only a small number of stories clearly written in the tradition of fairy tales. However, these stories – often beginning 'once upon a time' – were all written by girls. In the following narrative, written by a Year 4 girl, it is interesting to note that while the hero of the piece was the fairy, it is the King who appears to hold the power.

> Once upon a time a little princess had a happy life. She had every-thing she wanted. Christine the princess had nobody to talk to. One night she gotten ready for bed. But just after she went to sleep a witch and a mean wizard stole her and took her to a big castle where she would be trapped in a cage. [ ] the witch and the wizard gone to another kingdom and stole a prince called Simon and took him too. The witch began her potion. She began to flick through her books and finally she found it and said in a squeaky voice 'A tongue of a frog and a heart of a king, a teaspoon of ear wax and a pinch of sugar' and stirred it all in a big big pot. Christine's mother was very worried her father called the guards and said whoever finds the princess I will give them a pot of gold. The next day the guards set off to find her. Now Prince Simons mother and father didn't care about him they wanted him to go away they didn't love him since his little brother came along. Simon had to sleep in the basement while his brother slept in the biggest bedroom you ever seen. Simon was going to be

> eaten first. So the wizard said in a squeaky voice 'Get down boy' 'I can't' said Simon 'I afraid of heights I can't jump down.' So the wizard carried him down. While all this noise was going on a little fairy was listening behind the door and said to herself what a mean witch and wizard she made sure that they won't kill any more children. As the wizard was carrying Simon she pointed her wand and said ABRACADABRA The wizard blinked and put Simon down Simon and Christine were amazed. The witch said what are you doing the fairy pointed her wand again and said ABRACADABRA the witch blinked. So they went back to a castle and said sorry to the king. Simon lived with them and they all lived happily ever after.

Another Year 4 girl wrote the only 'love' story. In this story, while the children are transfixed by the magic of the wizard/plumber, the teacher, Miss Cradle, is more interested in the fact that the plumber is a 'hunk'. But this is not entirely a traditional love story as it is Miss Cradle (are the gentle, 'nursery' connotations of this name a coincidence?) who plots to 'get her man' and it is she who asks him to marry her. As a teacher, Miss Cradle is portrayed as the figure of authority; although it is the boys in this story who stereotypically are 'naughty': having 'had a row' from their teacher they dare not run into the water spraying from the broken radiator for a second time.

> One Monday morning in the town of Middlesex a small school were taking the register ... While Miss Cradle was taking the register there was a big crash! The radiator had fallen off the wall and water was squirting everywhere. Some of the boys ran into the spraying water but the teacher told them off. 'I'll call a plumber' said Miss Cradle. She ran to the phone and dialled the number with a thin boney finger. A few minutes later when the plumber arrived he didn't look like a plumber he had a long white beard, small round glasses, a long blue cloak with stars and moons on it and a hat to match. Everyone thought he looked more like a wizard than a plumber. Bob, Luje, Scott and Ray started laughing HE HE HE HA HA HA! Then the man starting talking in a strange language. Wizardy Way Wizardy Woo let the radiator be fixed for you and he left. Everyone stared in amazement. Everyone started to whisper. 'Well he was a hunk' said Miss Cradle. The big red bell rang it was twenty past three and all the children went home ... The next day in school Miss Cradle took the register. While Miss Cradle was taking the register a whisper was

going round the class … When the whisper died down Miss Cradle said I want you all to jump on the radiator. 'Are you feeling all right Miss Cradle' asked Carly sympathetically. I'm feeling all right thank you Carly' said Miss Cradle. So everyone climbed on the radiator. They jumped and jumped and jumped. Suddenly there was a big crash and water sprayed everywhere. The boys did not dare to run into the water after the row they had last time. Miss Cradle ran to the phone and dialled the number. In a few minutes the plumber arrived and before he stepped through the door she said 'Willyoumarryme' the plumber said 'yes'. So they got married and everyone lived happily ever after.

A Year 6 boy wrote a more brutal story of adult relationships. Despite its theme of betrayal, this is, in fact, an essentially moral tale. Paul, the main protagonist, is not portrayed as a hero and his actions are not condoned or glamorised by the writer. Indeed, it is the 'wronged' wife who, ridding herself of husband and his girlfriend, ultimately emerges as the victor.

Rescue

Paul was flash and flamboyant. He liked to go out with the lads or was it the lads? He was happily married [correction] married to Anna but he was having an affair with a woman called Julie! This had been going on for quite some time. Julie was a secretary. She enjoyed her work mostly because she got quite a bit of money. Anna also had a job as a postwoman. She also helped to be a lifeguard.

Anyway, one day Paul was walking on the beach. He fancied a swim so he got out his swimming things and went strait to swim. He was about midway in to his swim when something big and heavy hit him on the back of his head. He started to drown somebody raised the alarm. Anna was a lifeguard of course she heard about this and she grabbed the life ring. 'She swam as fast as she Linford' one passer by said when she rescued him he was unconscious. She managed to drag Paul back to safety he got whipped away in an ambulance.

The next day Julie was reading the paper when she stumbled across an article about Paul and he was in North Park hospital, She rush to the hospital. Meanwhile Anna was already there, When Julie got there she found the ward. When she got there Anna said 'who are you?' 'his girlfriend' 'I'm his wife' Anna started. Julie went to hit Anna but she slipped and she hit Paul instead and then the deadly beep sound beeeep. Paul was dead.

Julie was devastated so much that she decided to commit suicide. This is what she did on the 22nd March on North [ ] she jump and died.

Only one thing left to solve. Who threw the rock that hit Paul and that is quite simple. Anna did know about the affair and that's who threw the rock.

Boys' stories

The violence and death included in this narrative was, however, a common element of many of the boys' stories as the following passages illustrate. This was not apparent in any of the stories written by girls in the sample group.

Suddenly Scott heard a noise. These horrible scaley monster dragons came and locked us up and with a smirk on his face said you are breakfast tomorrow ...

(Year 5 boy)

... In the room there was a long table with blood on the table. In the back room we could see people killing people and people screaming and shouting ...

(Year 5/6 boy)

Suddenly there was an explosion and the engines exploded ... Unknown to me the engines were overheating ... they exploded and the plane crashed in the jungle.

(Year 5/6 boy)

... Steven ran to school got in class and the building collapsed onto the school and crushed everyone and Steven died.

(Year 6 boy)

Similarly, several of the boys' stories (and none of the girls' stories) included themes of patriotism and war. For example:

... Ding doing there's someone at the door. I'll go and answer it. Quickly move out of Britain now Germany is attacking move now ...

(Year 6 boy)

I tipped water over his head and I had a fight with him and I killed him and give him a black eye and a bleeding nose. United Kingdom wins and the world is back to normal ...

(Year 6 boy)

Fantasy land

Both boys' and girls' stories were often located in, or included a visit to, a fantasy world. In the boys' stories this fantasy world, without exception, provided a context of battles for power and domination. A Year 5 boy wrote the following story.

The deadly castle

I was walking home from school on a sunny Tuesday, I was quite sad because Scott and Andrew were missing. Soon I was by an old grey rotting castle. I was thinking silly but somehow I thought Scott and Andrew were in the castle. So I threw my bag over the gate and I followed. My knees were trembling I was so scared but I knew I had to go in. The door was locked but there was a broken window by the door. I jumped through the window. Luckily I had a project today that needed a torch so I got out of my bag a red and yellow torch that could shine from 100 metres away. I span around because I heard a noise. It was them, it was Scott and Andrew and behind them was goblins. I asked Scott who are they? He said they're the King bogey man slaves. They were hiding from the bogey men I joined them. The castle was huge and there was cobwebs and spiders The goblins were green with hats on their head. We all heard footsteps coming closer. Me, Scott, Andrew and the goblins hid in another place but we were surrounded by big, horrible, smelly bogey men. I thought it was a dream, I said someone pinch me.

Andrew pinched me but nothing happened so I knew it wasn't a dream. The goblins were caught. The bogey man king said 'who are you?' I said we are humans. They took us prisoners in this dungeon which had all rats in it but I didn't mind that, but I did mind the faces of the bogey. The first night I was a little scared because I didn't know if the bogey men would come in and shoot us. It was soon morning. Me and Scott were awake and Andrew was sleeping so we woke him up. He wasn't very pleased. The bogey man opened the door we all jumped on him and pinned him to the floor and shouted 'how do we get out of here'! His bright red eyes and plump body was scared but he managed to say 'there's a door just outside on the left, go through there and your out' We locked him in and went by the door. There were loads of bogey men. We beat them all up and freed the goblins. The goblins ran after us back to my house to live with us for ever and ever.

(Year 5 boy)

For the girls, the fantasy world was often a much less threatening place in which to be. For example:

All of a sudden I was in telly tubby land with my best friend Rachel. The first thing we saw was very unusual but true. Mr Blobby and the tubby tellys were having a tea party to celebrate la-las birthday ...

(Year 4/5 girl)

As this example shows, girls' stories were sometimes influenced by the television programmes they watched. This was also true of boys' stories – for example:

Space danger

We have our own space ship me Christopher and Richard and Max were on an adventure to seek out new life and new civilisation to where no one been before. We landed on a planet and there the alien hunter [ ] call themselves Dracks. They were monsters with red eyes. And a spikey tail [ ] . We took samples of their blood and samples of the planet. The samples were made of acid and one of my assistance touched the blood and melted. She changed into a Drack and kill the cop. Richard kill her. The samples were actually a disease and a plague...

(Year 5 boy)

Heroes and heroines?

I noted above that it has been suggested that girls often write their stories in the third person. This was not found to be the case in this study: while a small number of stories were written in the third person by both girls and boys, most stories were written in the first person. One noticeable gender difference, however, was that boys' stories often contained an independent and powerful central character. For example a Year 5/6 boy began his story:

The lucky break-in

'Smash' the glass went and these people with black hats on broke into the Alliance and Leicester bank. I'm the boss of the whole Alliance and Leicesters in Great Britain. I take care of everybody in the bank ...

In addition, the writer, as central character, was often the hero of the story, succeeding where others had failed! Another Year 5/6 boy ended his story:

... When we were on our way I said to Richard let's go back and find out who killed Rose then they could be arrested for murder. We telephoned the police they tried for five months looking for the murderer. But they couldn't find he or she who killed Rose. So Richard and I went to see if we could solve the case. After a week Richard and I found the man who killed Rose and he was arrested for life and once again Richard and I went home.

In the girls' stories the central character often asked for the help of a stronger male – even where there appeared to be little need. For example:

... I saw a island I went on it. It was full of trees I had a look around. It was lots of pebbles. I picked the pebbles and I built a house and I got help. The sailor shouted do you want help. I shouted yes please ...

(Year 4 girl)

The following story by a Year 3 girl vividly illustrates this point. Despite rescuing a baby from a burning building and putting out the blazing fire, the main character, Superwoman, still needs Superman to give his approval of her actions and to take her back to the safety of her home: it is thus Superman who is portrayed as the real hero.

The pink drink

I had just walked into my local shop when I saw a bright pink can. It was a strange drink that I had never seen before called pinky minky. I had to buy it ... When I drank it (it) turned me into Superwoman. I went to save a burning building. When I went there there was some(one) saying my baby (is in) the burning building. I ask her which room she (said) the tenth floor. I fly up there as fast as I can. I saved the poor baby and took (her) to her mother. She (said) thank you Superwoman. I said no problem. But who's going to put the fire out? I will I said. So I took a deep breath and blow as hard as I could. I said no fear Superwoman is here but when I wasn't looking I bumped into a lamppost and lost all my power and turn back into a little girl. I said what an amazing adventure but how am I going to get home? Then I saw something in the sky. It was Superman. He said that was a very brave (thing) you done. So remember you (will) always be Superwoman and don't forget it. I said thank you Superman. But now I want to go home I said.

Action or interaction?

It was also apparent that the boys' narratives tended to be 'action-packed' in a way that girls' narratives were not. In addition, the language of comics and cartoons was often used as part of this action – and as in cartoons, the main character (a boy) was usually portrayed as virtually indestructible. This is illustrated in the following story by a Year 4 boy:

Up, up and away!

I was strolling along when I suddenly tripped over a stone 'whaooo!' I moaned as I fell, I hit the ground with a thump! I got up and saw what seemed to be a giant picnic basket. I walked closer and it was a hot air balloon, I got in it but it wasn't secured to the ground properly and got lifted off the ground. I looked over the side and saw I was about 3000 metres I fainted. When I recovered I got out of the balloon (because it had landed in a thorn bush) and my foot just missed a thorn, I jumped and landed on a road. I picked a newspaper it read: 'today a UFO was spotted flying across Miami Dam' some people said they saw a boy in there. I looked at the photo 'hey that's my balloon!' I shouted, then before I could walk away reporters and photographers were crowding round me. I said 'get lost and bother someone else, just leave me in peace' They said 'grrrr' and walked away 'peace at last' I said. Suddenly the wind blew my balloon and I went drifting away. I flew across the USA and the basket of the balloon got caught on the top of the Empire State Building. I fell and fell until poof! I felt as if I fell off a plane and landed on a bouncy castle. I was in a state of shock because I fell 2000 storeys. I got up and shook my head, I had landed on a trampoline. I walked around the city of New York and on the floor was a M16. (an M16 if you didn't know is a very powerful weapon and in this case it was loaded) I picked up the M16 and tried it out. Boom! 'Oh so it's not an M16 its even better a grenade launcher' I shouted. I walked on until suddenly 'freeze' a voice commanded. I turned round and Boom! Boom! Boom! Boom! And 'whaaaa' 'Nice one, gross' I said then I spotted an artillery shop. I went and said ' a shot gun and I'll have a golden gun and a klobb? oh I mustn't forget a KF7 soviet'. Tring! 'That'll be £1,000' said the storekeeper. 'Here I'll write a cheque' Scribble, scribble went my pen, rrriiippp 'here' I said 'thanks good day'. I pulled out my klobb then I met a man of about ninety three and he was being sarcastic to everyone who passed so like or[?] I would do I shot him then suddenly wewawwewaw it was a police car. 'Give up' they said 'no!' I yelled bbbb rrrrr went my klbb suddenly a police man sneaked up behind me then 'your nicked your lubbering piece 'o' junk' they took me into custody and they said 'forty years in the slammer for you'. So I was locked away for forty or maybe more years, I hope I get out.

The girls' narratives often moved at a slower pace; they focused not so much on the action as the interaction between the main characters. In the following story (also entitled 'Up, up and away!') the cliff top rescue is almost incidental to the story line. And despite this rescue we see again that the main protagonists (girls) are not portrayed as self-sufficient heroes. Rather, they are vulnerable children lost in a world without adults to keep them safe (note that the reason Joanne is on the cliff top is because she has lost her mummy). There is nothing they can do but to wait passively for their air-balloon adventure to run its course. And what do they do in the two hours they are waiting? Sit and chat, of course!

Up, up and away!

One scalding evening in March after school I was playing with my friends Rachel and Jenna in the park. The park seemed very quiet. Just then we saw a gigantic hot air balloon. We all went up to it and I said 'Let's get in!' 'Right' 'Jenna you unravel the knot then hop in and we'll be off'. So she undid the knot, hopped in and sure enough we were up upon the silky white clouds. As we were sinking through the clouds Jenna began to cough badly because she had asthma. I give her pump back to her because I was minding it for her because she didn't have any pockets. When she had it she was fine, but Rachel said 'look we are sinking down very quick, it looks as if we are going to crash'. 'Oh no' I said then Jenna 'everybody keep calm and then we should be safe'. Rachel said 'oh my goodness I knew we shouldn't of come up here' but then we started slowing down. We were about 40 feet from the ground then we saw Joanne on a cliff she had lost her mummy. She said 'boy am I glad to see you girls'. 'Jump in' we said so we all sat down and had a chat. After a couple of hours we felt a BIG BUMP. Joanne said 'We have landed' so we got out and we dropped Jo off and went home. Rachel promised herself that she would never take anything that did not belong to her!

(Year 4/5 girl)

Detail, description and dialogue

In their stories it appeared that the girls were also more likely to include detail and description. Moreover, in contrast to the boys' emphasis on the dangerous and daring, the girls' descriptions often referred to the safe, the happy and the beautiful. The following is an excerpt from a story by a Year 3 girl:

... I ended up on a beautiful island. I saw on the island a lovely waterfall and a beautiful meadow with loads of wonderful creatures and flowers. I thought it was beautiful. I couldn't believe I was here to see all these things. I love it here I said then I saw a wood it was full of green trees and squirrels and rabbits, foxes, birds and grass and the sun was coming out. I was really happy now ...

This is not to say that all the boys' stories relied on action at the expense of description, as this excerpt from a story by a Year 4 boy demonstrates:

Abracadabra

'Hey Bob catch' shouted Joe across the lawn. He threw the frisbee it skimmed across the lush green grass and hit Bob's trainers with a loud thud. 'Boring' 'Huh' 'This is boring' he repeated. 'What shall we do then?' 'How about going for a walk?' 'OK then.' 'Where shall we go?' In the end the twins decided to go up the hill an excellent choice although they didn't know it. The purple heather brushed against the twins legs. Suddenly they came to a fairly large opening in the ground ... They walked through the cave. They were met by a dim candle that lit a chamber. Both brothers jumped as they heard a voice. The room was filled with pots, jars and tubes of all types, sizes and colours ... The man had a bushy beard down to his waist. 'Hello' he said 'I'm Ozwald!' 'Call me Oz for short!' He flashed Bob a friendly grin. Bob realised his mouth was gaping open. He shut it instantly.

Among the sample group, both boys and girls used dialogue to enliven their stories although within the writing samples it was clear that this had been a teaching focus in several Key Stage 2 classes. In addition, there were examples of both boys' and girls' stories which included some reference to emotions – although in the boys' stories this tended to be feeling scared before the central character eventually overcame the danger or feeling angry before calming down. Similarly, pain is referred to by boys as something fairly fleeting or transient; it, too, could be overcome in a short space of time. The following excerpt by a Year 4 boy illustrates this:

... My friend was trying to get me out but then he ran away because he saw a tiger with vicious teeth going to bite me. He bit off my leg and the pain was really really painful. I was screaming and crying until the pain cooled down about ten minutes later ...

Dealing with danger

Girls also made reference to emotions, often to feeling scared. But unlike the boys, difficulties were not resolved through, for example, confronting and overcoming the aggressor. Rather, as the following examples make clear, the girls tended to defuse or transform the object of their fear.

> ... Then a terrible feeling struck my head. How was I going to get home from the island. I thought I was going to die from thirst but I wasn't. I started to cry but I was OK. I had just found something to keep me alive. It was a coconut tree it had loads of juicy ones that I'd love to eat. I thought I would be the only one on the island when I saw some pirates they had red hats and a black eye patch and one even had a parrot which had green read and yellow wings It was lovely. Then all of a sudden I thought they were going to fight me but they were kind pirates and asked if they could help.
>
> (Year 3 girl)

> Inside the castle I could hear a deep voice I thought it must be a giant so I went up to have a look. The giant said I can see you. I stated to shake but it was too late the giant was already out in the garden so I asked him his name. 'George he replied.' I asked him if he knew anything about the missing spoon. ... George asked me if I'd be his friend.
>
> (Year 6 girl)

> Then the witch walked away because she was a kind witch all the time. She didn't kill anyone before so she was a kind witch all the time and the witch shouted bye I see you agen.
>
> (Year 5/6 girl)

Conclusion

What, then, did I discover about the content of the children's narratives? In many ways, this exploration confirmed the findings of previous studies: the narratives reflected the different worlds in which the boys and girls lived. Boys' stories were often (but not always) action-packed fantasies of violence and domination incorporating the language and sound effects of the cartoons and videos they enjoyed. Girls, on the other hand, tended to write about friends and relationships, their stories moved at a slower place and incorporated more detail and description. In their stories, boys often positioned themselves as powerful and independent; girls positioned themselves as vulnerable and dependent.

Narrative is, after all, a way of reflecting on experiences and making sense of these (Laycock 1996). We should not be surprised, therefore, that boys and girls use story writing as a way of working out and displaying their gender identity. Moreover, it is likely that, as they were more eager to please, girls tried to identify and conform to what they believed their teacher wanted: 'nice', happy stories full of detail and description. Boys, on the other hand, were not so bothered about teachers' expectations: they wrote stories for themselves.

Having examined the children's writing, the teachers began to collaborate on planning aspects of work that they wanted to explore for themselves. But it was also decided that an important voice was missing from this early work, that of the children themselves. What did the children have to tell us about the teaching and learning of literacy? This is the focus of Chapter 6.

6 Children talking about literacy
Out of the mouths of babes

By this point in the project, it was apparent that any ideas we may have had about finding a simple 'solution' to the boys and literacy issue had been naïve. Indeed, the more we 'peeled back the layers', the more complexities we exposed and the more questions there were to be asked. Such is the way of school-based action research.

As the teachers began to collaborate in the planning of their next move – what action they wanted to take – it was suggested that in gathering evidence an important 'voice' was missing: that of the children themselves. I therefore arranged to talk to the 'sample' children and to find out what they had to say about literacy in the primary school. I was interested, for example, in how they defined and identified good readers and writers; their perceived difficulties with narrative writing; and also, what advice they would give to their teachers about the teaching of literacy.

READING

Reading outside school

In order to sharpen the focus on the teaching and learning of literacy *in* school, I initially asked the children about their experiences of literacy, and the development of particular literacy skills, *outside* school. For example, the children were asked about the reading habits of their 'parents' – that is, the adults living in their house. The younger children appeared to consider their parents' reading preferences and habits in terms of what their parents read to them. Here again, gender stereotypes were evident. For example, in response to the question 'Do your mummy and daddy like reading?', children in the reception class commented:

G: Yes ... and my bampa.
B: My daddy doesn't.
G: My mother likes reading *Barbie*.
B: My daddy likes reading *Pinocchio*.

B: My mummy likes reading the paper.
G: My mammy likes reading *The Spice Girls*.
B: My daddy likes reading *Pinocchio*.
B: My daddy likes reading ... my books.

[In the dialogue in this chapter, B = boy, G = girl]

Many of the Key Stage 2 children maintained that their parents mainly read newspapers and magazines, although they indicated that it was their mothers who were 'more likely' to read novels. In terms of the content of their reading the children again echoed gender stereotypes: they maintained that their fathers read magazines or books about fishing, the army and football while their mothers were more interested in reading about 'people'. For example, the Year 4 children commented:

G: My mother always has a newspaper ... she likes reading that. And after school she always buys a magazine ... same as my Auntie. They reads newspapers and magazines so they won't miss out ...
G: And my mother does.
B: No-one in my house likes reading.
B: My mother reads anything ... because she is a teacher.
G: My mother reads newspapers and magazines and my father reads football magazines ...
B: My father likes Elton John books.
G: I forgot to mention that my mother doesn't really read ... she reads the exciting bits but she usually does the crossword.

Similarly, the sample group in Amanda's (Year 5/6) class maintained:

B: My mother tells me to go down the shop and get an *Evening Post* and she reads that.
G: My father reads the paper ...
G: My mother and father reads the newspaper ...
G: My mother reads magazines and my father reads the newspaper ... sometimes my mother reads a book ... you know, when they tells you about people ...
B: My mother and her friend reads the newspaper ... sometimes my mother will read a novel ...
B: My mother reads poetry ...
B: My father's girlfriend reads magazines ...
B: My mother does all the crosswords.
G: I flick through the newspaper ...
B: Yes, I do sometimes.

About half of the Key Stage 1 children maintained that other family members – mothers, fathers and siblings – read to them or with them. At the lower end of Key Stage 2 home reading of this kind appeared to be very limited and by the time the children reached Year 6 it was non-existent. What was more interesting, perhaps, was the type of stories children maintained they most enjoyed listening to. As well as fairy tales, and stories about magic and monsters, several children referred to stories their parents had 'made up'. For example, one girl in Gaynor's (Year 1/2) class commented: 'I liked the story about when my mammy went sailing when she was a little girl', while a boy maintained: 'I liked it when daddy told me about the white shark when he was diving.'

In terms of their own 'home reading', both boys and girls commented that they liked reading comics and magazines; boys, in particular, referred to football magazines. In addition, both boys and girls maintained that they enjoyed adventure and fantasy/horror books such as Harry Potter and Goosebumps – 'because you never know what's coming round the corner' (Year 4 girl) – with Roald Dahl being mentioned most often as a 'favourite author'. However, as they got older, it appeared that children (boys and girls) were less likely to read books: rather, like their parents, they tended to read comics, magazines and newspapers. In addition, their reading tended to be functional: for example, for 'finding out what's on television' (Year 6 girl) or 'finding out the times of the tides' (Year 5/6 boy).

Reading in school

If children were not always positive about reading at home, then they were even less enthusiastic about reading in school. Many of the older children claimed that the books in their class libraries were 'boring'. Children in the Year 5/6 class, for example, commented:

B: I'd rather colour in and do drawing.
B: If it's a book I don't enjoy I don't read it … I just flick through it.
B: I don't like many of the books in our class …
G: … because we've read them all.
B: I want to read *Danny Champion of the World* …
B: There's a film coming out about that …
B: I only like reading *My Granny was a Sumo Wrestler* …
B: In my class we've read them all before … I gets a bit bored.

But it was the stress associated with 'silent reading' time that the Key Stage 2 children complained about most. For example, the Year 4 children stated:

G: I don't like silent reading because, there's loads of people around you and in your house … there's peace.

G: And if you gets a word you don't know ... and other people know it I gets jealous because I don't ...

B: I don't like reading anywhere except in hotels ... I don't know why ... In the jacuzzi I read ten pages ...

G: I don't like reading in school because everyone's so silent and I like to read out loud ... in your house everybody's talking and you feel cosy and in school everybody's so silent it feels like you're on your own and I don't like feeling on my own.

Children in Year 3 class also commented:

B: We does quiet reading twice a day in the classroom.

G: I don't like it much because sometimes I get stuck on the words and you're not allowed to go and ask Miss ...

G: And you're not allowed to talk to your friends ...

G: It's like your mouth dries up because you can't talk to your friends ... otherwise you might lose a star.

G: And then you lets all your friends down and then you feel really angry ... and all your friends say 'Oh brilliant one, now you've lost a star for us.'

When asked whether they preferred reading fiction or non-fiction books in school (for the younger children I used the terms 'stories' and 'finding-out books'), most children were non-committal: tending to answer either 'both' or, more often at Key Stage 2, 'neither'. Moreover, when asked what non-fiction book they had recently 'looked at' in class, both boys and girls referred to books about, for example, bodies, animals, dinosaurs, space and 'true ghost stories' (!)

WRITING

Writing stories

From the initial phase of this research I was aware that story writing was the form of writing that teachers maintained caused the most difficulties for children. It was also the form of writing that they least liked to teach. When talking to the children I was therefore particularly interested in exploring their perceptions, expectations and concerns about writing stories. For example, the children were asked to comment on how they thought their teachers judged 'good' story writing. It appeared that as they moved up through the school, children's perceptions of teachers' expectations in this respect (and the children's own concerns?) not only changed but grew incrementally. The youngest children referred essentially to the importance of handwriting and quantity.

Reception

G: You've got to write nice ...
G: And little letters ...
B: If you scribble she rubs it out.

Reception/Year 1

B: When we do our letters right ...
B: And do loads of pages ...

Year 1/2

G: C and J write the best stories because they write lots of pages ...
B: And G because the writing's neat.
B: I've learned to write little writing now.

The Year 2, 3 and 4 children also thought handwriting and length was important. In addition, they referred to the importance of punctuation and grammar as well as the inclusion of humour and excitement.

Year 2

G: J writes long stories and he spells them right ...
B: Before he's written two pages.
B: I've written three pages once.
B: When he's really neat he don't get a sweet or nothing, does he?
G: A good story has good things in it ...
B: ... like full stops.
B: My dragon story had lots of excitement in it ... Because in the beginning they couldn't see the dragon, they just heard noises.

Year 3

B: My teacher likes funny ones ...
G: ... and neat handwriting ...
B: ... no mistakes ...
B: ... good ideas ...
G: ... and no really small handwriting so she can't read it ...
G: ... not really big and big.

Year 4

G: My teacher's looking for good sense in your ideas ... long words ...
B: Full stops and capital letters ...
B: ... like hard words ...

G: And not too many 'ands' ...
G: She hates too many 'ands'.
G: Spelling and capital letters are important.
B: Yes, capital letters and full stops. Because if you don't remember capital letters and full stops she makes us do it again.

In giving their perceptions of teachers' judgements, the oldest Key Stage 2 children emphasised additional factors: for example, the inclusion of detail and description, the use of paragraphs as well as the importance of 'a good plot'.

Year 5

B: My teacher likes descriptive writing. Like if you went into a castle, describe everything in the castle.
B: Punctuation ...
B: ... full stops ...
B: ... how adventurous it was ...
G: ... spelling.

Year 5/6

B: Capital letter, full stops.
G: Paragraphs.
B: Describing words.
G: Exciting ... adventurous.
G: Lots of describing words. Making the sentence sound busy.
G: See Miss, if you were talking about a house in the middle and nobody went in she wouldn't like 'There was a house in the centre of the street and nobody went in it'; she would like something like 'There was a creepy old house with creepy windows ... '

Year 6

B: Well paragraphed, sentences, full stops, capital letters ...
B: Well described.
B: Long words.
B: Good description, describing things in detail ... Describe everything in detail ...
G: I always forgets paragraphs though ...
G: ... spelling ...
B: ... and a good story ... a good plot.
B: A long one ... over two pages.
B: You've got to write about something really happening ...
G: ... and handwriting.

G: She doesn't like 'and then I went' ... She doesn't like 'and then ... and then ... and then' ...

G: We did that work ... B, what was it called when we did that work on 'because' and 'so'?

B: Oh, connecting words.

TM: And did that help with writing stories?

ALL: No!

Difficulties with story-writing

I was also interested in the children's opinions about their difficulties with story writing. The children in the youngest classes mentioned the physical effort of writing, such as pencil control. For example:

> Like if you're not holding it ... well, your hand goes wiggly ...
>
> (G: Reception/Year1)

> When you just come in you don't know what hand you're writing with and it gets smaller and smaller.
>
> (B: Reception/Year 1)

From Year 1/2, spelling was also mentioned; as one boy commented: 'It's hard to spell Godzilla!'

However, for all the children, regardless of age or gender, it was the problem of 'ideas' which appeared to be their major concern. For example, children commented:

G: Sometimes you can't think of anything ... then you just write a story about something ...

(Reception/Year 1)

B: ... It's always hard to think of things to write.

G: The hardest thing is thinking of ideas ... because everyone's noisy and everyone's looking for ideas and it gives you a headache.

(Year 2)

G: Sometimes it's hard to think of the danger bits.

(Year 1/2)

B: Sometimes I sit for ten minutes trying to think ... and then it's playtime.

(Year 5)

Concentration and 'holding on to these ideas' were also cited as problems by both boys and girls. For example, a Year 4 girl commented that:

> You've got to keep the words in your mind ... I either write words twice or I'll write the same sentence again ... or I'll make it so it doesn't make sense ... '

Similarly, children from the Year 3 class maintained:

B: I always forgets about what I'm writing.
G: It's like you're writing and then you're talking to a friend and then you forgets about it ... and then I don't know what to write any more.

For some children the problem seemed to be not so much thinking of an idea but deciding which of their many ideas they were 'going to stick with'. One Year 4 girl explained:

> I think writing stories is quite hard actually because I'll write with the ideas I've got in my head and then I'll stop and my hand's hurting and like ... you think of so many ideas and then you want to change your story ...

Several Key Stage 2 children maintained that their main difficulty was getting the ideas down on paper. For some children this was linked to the physical demands of writing:

> I think writing stories is difficult because you don't have enough time and you have to write and write and you get so many ideas in your head and you keep writing and your hand starts to hurt ... And Miss says, 'Don't worry, it will stop now' and so you waits and waits and then ... you just runs out of time.
>
> (Year 4 girl)

For others the difficulty was one of expressing ideas in sentences: a Year 5 boy commented, for example: 'I've got the ideas, but it's trying to put it into sentences. It's putting it into sentences that's the problem.'

Whose stories?

Another difficulty referred to by Key Stage 2 children related to their teachers' choice of story title. Children listed (with astounding accuracy!) the titles their teachers commonly provided: a Year 4 girl for example, commented that:

Most of the time she [the teacher] gives us titles like 'the mystery journey' or 'lost in the forest' ...

But the children maintained that even though they struggled to think of 'good ideas' these titles actually made story writing more difficult. A Year 4 boy commented:

I prefer writing my own stories because you've got a free mind ... You don't have to put down what Mrs G says.

A Year 6 boy explained:

The teacher asks us to write about 'the treasure island', 'the magic keys' ... stuff like that. And there's nothing different to write ... Like treasure island ... it's all been wrote before.

Children indicated that, in their view, being allowed to choose their own story titles would have a positive effect on their attainment. One girl in Amanda's class (Year 5/6) commented:

The worst thing is when you've got to write a story and they tells you ... the title has got to be 'the rescue' or something ... because if you've got to write what the teacher says it's boring and you haven't got any good ideas. It's more exciting if you've got your own title. You get down to it more.

Several children (boys and girls) maintained that not being able to write their 'own' stories contributed to their lack of enthusiasm for writing in school. For example, a boy in Amanda's (Year 5/6) class maintained:

I hate writing stories in school. If we were allowed to chose our own titles it would be all right. When I go to bed I don't go to bed ... I put my lamp on and writes stories.

And what they wanted to write about, children maintained, was their own reality:

About yourself. Because you knows about it. You've done it yourself. You know what happened.

(Year 4 boy)

Initial planning

Planning was recognised by teachers as an important part of story writing. In Chapter 4 I noted that the teachers had commented that it was in the discussion that preceded written work that gender differences were particularly apparent. In this situation it was the boys who generally came up with 'best' ideas. The children in the Reception/Year 1 classes disagreed over who suggested the best ideas for stories – overall the girls maintained that it was the girls and the boys that it was the boys. The Year 2 children took a different view, however. They commented:

B: On the carpet the girls are all quiet and the boys are giving more ideas.
G: That's because the girls can't think of ideas.
B: Because the boys have more imagination.

The older children generally supported this assertion. This appeared to be related to the boys' domination of classroom discussions. For example, the children from Christine's class commented:

TM: Who do you think suggests the best ideas for stories?
ALL: Boys.
B: Boys have got more imaginations.
B: Girls have got Barbies in their heads.
G: I don't like Barbies ...
B: ... Yes, Barbies and pop and things.
TM: So what do you [boy] have in your head?
B: Football.
B: Yeah, football.
G: I like football.
TM: What makes you think the boys have better ideas?
B: We just know. Because the girls sit there silently and the boys are jumping up and things.

However, many boys and girls commented on their reluctance to articulate their ideas during the planning sessions 'on the carpet'. For some boys this reluctance was due to competition – 'other people might pinch your ideas' (Year 4) – while for the girls it appeared to be related more to a lack of confidence: 'I get embarrassed talking about my ideas' (Year 5). The children explained that this was because:

G: The boys make fun of the girls ...
B: ... Call them names and things.

(Year 5)

Planning sheets

From my interviews with the teachers I was aware that following the class discussion, children were asked to complete a planning sheet; this was designed to encourage the children to consider the plot and characters in some detail before starting to write. These sheets included boxes in which children were encouraged to note down the beginning, middle and ending of their story as well as providing space for them to outline the main characters, the context and the dilemma. The planning sheets received almost unanimous condemnation from pupils: only children in one Year 5 class admitted that: planning sheets *were* helpful 'because you can write your ideas down'.

The vast majority of children maintained that using a planning sheet was *not* the way they wrote stories; rather, the Year 4 girls maintained:

G: You think about your ideas ... and make it up ... as you're going along.
G: On your planning sheet you put down one set of ideas ... but when you come to write your stories you've got a whole new set of ideas.

The children in Amanda's (Year 5/6) class also commented:

G: The planning sheet ... that's the worst part of the story.
TM: Why?
G: Because it takes up too much time.
B: I write it and then I forgets it.
B: It worns you out.
B: You've got to write it out properly ... and by the time you've done that your hand's aching.
B: I don't reckon there's any point in doing it because we only rush through it ... and then don't even look at it ... I bet you any money that everybody who uses a planning sheet they don't even look at it ... they just write it to keep the teacher happy and then put it in the bin.
B: That's what I does. I writes on it then just puts it to one side and carries on ... I don't bother with the planning sheets ...
G: It's a waste of time.
B: Say Miss gives us an hour to do it all, it takes us nearly an hour to fill in the planning sheet and we don't have time to write the story.
B: He's exaggerating.
G: I would prefer to use a rough book ... just jot things down.

Nor did children always appreciate teachers trying to structure their story writing in other ways. Boys in Simon's (Year 5) class, for example, commented:

B: Our teacher asked us to write ... when we go in this rocket ... been to another planet. Sir gave us the first line of each part.

B: That made it harder ...

B: Yeah, because we had to fit in with what *he* wanted.

Stress

Time – specifically a lack of time to complete a story – appeared to be a key source of anxiety for both boys and girls. One Year 4 girl commented:

> I worry about time ... my teacher says ... 'Yes, five minutes to finish now ... five minutes to finish'. And like, I'm just starting my story ...

Another Year 4 boy commented:

> I keep looking at the clock ... Miss always goes like this ... 'You're going to have to speed up because you're too slow.' It makes your tummy go round ... I start to sweat ... I'm looking at the clock and thinking 'I'm wasting time, I'm wasting time, I'm wasting time ... '

A further source of stress identified by children was when they recognised for themselves that the story they had written was not 'their best work'. Children in Paula's (Year 3) class maintained:

G: If you think your writing's really bad you know you're not going to get a star ... like if you've rubbed out too much.

B: ... if there's lots of mistakes ... you feel ...

B: It's like your heart's punching ...

G: You sweat ... things like that.

Writing in other forms

In phase one of this project, teachers had maintained that all the children enjoyed reading, writing and listening to poetry. When questioned the children agreed that they did, indeed, enjoy reading and listening to poetry, but, for the children in Years 5 and 6 in particular, it appeared that *writing* poetry was another matter!

The children in Years 3 and 4 maintained that while writing poems was challenging, they *were* easier to write than stories. This was because:

> You can make them as long or as short as you want. With stories Mrs G makes us write one, two or three pages but with poems you don't even have to write a page ... maybe a quarter page ...

> (Year 4 girl)

This child added 'And you don't have to write in sentences!' Another Year 4 girl commented: 'With a poem ... you can put words together that don't make sense.'

However, the children in Years 5 and 6 maintained that writing poetry 'was really hard'. One Year 6 girl commented:

> I don't mind sitting on the carpet listening to poetry but when he makes us go and write a poem he makes it too difficult.

These 'difficulties' included 'setting it out right' and 'sometimes getting words to rhyme'. In addition, a major problem highlighted by both boys and girls was the use of figurative language. For example: 'It's hard because you've got to put in loads of describing words' (Year 5/6 girl) and 'He [the teacher] says you're *still* not using enough adjectives' (Year 5/6 boy).

It may be significant that Years 5 and 6 were taught poetry by the same teacher. It may also be of significance that these children commented on their immense sense of pride at their completed work: the children in one class were keen show me a book that contained their 'best' poems.

TM: Do you like writing poetry?
ALL: No.
TM: No?
B: Mr T does! (*Laughter*)
B: Mr T reads us loads of poetry, man.
B: I likes reading them but I don't like writing them.
G: Mr T's got a book with all our poems in.
B: It's good, man.
B: That's one we wrote on the wall over there in the hall ... the dream team football one. Do you want to see it?

And what about children's attitudes towards writing in other forms? When interviewed, the teachers had suggested that the children were generally more enthusiastic about non-narrative than narrative writing. Many children indicated that this was, indeed, the case. Year 6 children commented, for example:

G: I prefer doing the other things.
G: Because it's shorter.
B: Because we get ... like if we pretend to be a news reporter we get to go round loads of places.
G: It's easier.
TM: What's easier about it?
G: You can use shorter words ...
B: It's not as strict as sitting in a classroom writing silently.

However, this view was not shared by all the children interviewed. Nor did the children appear to conform to gender stereotypes in this respect. For example, one Year 4 girl stated:

> I prefer to write reports. Because you've been there. If you have write stories then you have to think of ideas. But if you write reports you know what happened.

A Year 4 boy disagreed. He stated:

> I like writing stories. I don't like writing things that are true. I like reading facts and things but I don't like writing about them.

Advice for teachers

Towards the end of the interview, children were asked what advice they would give their teachers to encourage children to write 'better stories'. Unsurprisingly, perhaps, the Key Stage 2 children maintained that they should be allowed to write from their own experiences. In addition, the children again commented that the teachers should 'scrap' the planning sheets. A further area of agreement concerned the approach teachers should adopt when children were writing. The children in the Key Stage 2 classes maintained that constantly reminding them there were only so many minutes left to finish their stories was not helpful and merely served to 'raise their stress level'. Rather, the children maintained:

G: Don't push too hard … let them have as much time as they need.
G: And if you think the story needs a bit more work then talk to them … like a serious conversation.
G: I think they should let them write their own stories for once and if they don't think they're doing good with that then give them a title. And then give them ideas and ask them, 'Do you think this is too hard for you?' And if they say 'yes' then try and push it down a little bit so it's an easier title … so you can write an easier story.

(Year 4)

G: If we're stuck, don't say, 'Carry on and try your best' but sit by us and talk about it. That helps.
B: And if we're really slow behind let us give the idea to the teacher and she writes it down for us on a bit of paper.

(Year 5/6)

Differences in attainment and behaviour

A final area of interest was children's comments about the relative attainment and behaviour of boys and girls in school. In the Key Stage 1 classes, while the children maintained that they were all 'good workers', differences in behaviour were noted. For example, one boy in the Reception/Year 1 class boasted 'the boys are stronger than the girls, mind' and that 'they have to tells us [the boys] off because we always fights'. Similarly, children in Emma's (Year 2) class maintained:

G: Our teacher thinks we are *all* good writers.
B: The girls are better behaved.
TM: Are they?
G: Yes.
B: There's more boys like C … they're always fighting … push each other over.

By Year 3 gender stereotypes appeared to be even more obvious:

B: The best behaved is the girls.
G: Yes, they are.
G: Yes, the boys are fussy.
G: The girls get on with their work.
G: The girls work harder.
B: The boys are best though because we've got two brainy boys in our class.

Similarly, a conversation with Year 4 children echoed teachers' perceptions of boys' and girls' relative attainment in literacy. In addition, it also reflected gender stereotypes in terms of subject areas (even if these are no longer reflected in SATs results).

G: Girls write better stories … they think a bit more. The boys would do a page and the girls two or three pages. Most of the girls are quite good at reading. The girls have got one or two good readers and the rest are in the middle and the boys have got either good readers or not good readers … no middle.
B: Boys are better at sports.
B: Boys are best at history and maths, science it's about fifty-fifty.
G: Boys are better at maths because they go just like that and they've got the right answers. Girls have to think a bit.

DISCUSSION AND CONCLUSIONS

So what can be made of this data? In Chapter 4 I noted that, in the first phase of this research, the teachers had articulated stereotypical views of boys' attitudes towards and attainment in writing. However, we saw in Chapter 5 that the analysis of children's writing did not fully support teachers' perceptions: gender differences were less apparent than teachers had anticipated – particularly in relation to transcription skills. This third phase of the research again indicated that gender differences were not as great as teachers had initially supposed: the boys and girls in this study appeared to face many common difficulties in learning the skills of literacy. For example, boys and girls had similar perceptions about what counts as effective teaching and how their teachers identify good readers and writers. Boys and girls were also united in their dislike of silent reading and planning sheets, and in their desire to write their own stories. They both enjoyed (or did not enjoy) reading non-fiction as well as fiction, while by the end of Key Stage 2 their reading tended to be almost exclusively for utilitarian purposes. Significantly, perhaps, boys as well as girls commented on their difficulty with 'ideas' when writing stories. (Does this indicate there is a difference between suggesting ideas in a whole-class discussion and developing these ideas into a story while working on your own?)

Where there were gender differences these appeared to relate to two broad areas. The first of these was 'interests': that is, what boys and girls wanted to read and write about. In many respects the children conformed to gender stereotypes. But whereas boys were vociferous in decrying what they described as 'girls' interests' and 'girls' stories', in general, the girls were not so constrained. At Key Stage 2, for example, as well as the stereo-typical 'pop, boys and Barbies', girls maintained that they *also* enjoyed reading and writing about what were seen as boys' topics: adventure, football, computers, etc. The observation that girls have a less restrictive gender identity was highlighted in Chapter 2 and, as we saw, can be explained in relation to a number of gender theories. The extent to which the breadth and flexibility of gender identity might impact on children's attainment in literacy, however, is less clear and may be worthy of further exploration.

The second broad area of difference related to attitudes. The children involved in this research supported their teachers' perceptions that compared with the boys, the girls were often self-conscious and embarrassed, wanted to please the teacher and were more compliant. Boys, on the other hand, tended to be dominant and competitive, were more willing to take risks, and were less likely to do what they did not want to do. Indeed, it was apparent that the children could identify their teachers' values, expectations and judgements with outstanding accuracy.

But is this so surprising? Children desire to gain control of the worlds in which they live, and the world of school is no exception. In order to survive, children need quickly to learn what is deemed significant and appropriate not only as a pupil but, as I noted in Chapter 2, as a male or female pupil. It appears that female pupils tend to be rewarded for listening and doing as they are told while male pupils are rewarded for being 'funny' and assertive. However, whilst conveying and enforcing messages about 'good' girls being compliant and docile, it may be, as I suggested in Chapter 4, that teachers actually admire the 'sparkle' and challenge of boys and prefer to teach them. If this is the case, girls would appear to be in a no-win situation. It may be that, while in school, some stereotypically male characteristics have a negative impact on boys' attainment in English; for example, difficulties with concentration may mean that boys miss out on learning important literacy skills. But the significance of these characteristics in relation to success in the 'real' world is another matter. If teachers do endorse girls' passivity – and, as we saw in Chapter 5, the teachers in this study acknowledged that this was often the case – ultimately, are we educating boys or girls for failure?

While the specific focus of this research was on boys' difficulties with literacy, I was also interested in what children had to say in more general terms about the teaching and learning of literacy in school. The children's responses highlighted the complexity of their developing literacy skills and, in particular, of learning to write stories. As I noted above, children referred to their difficulties with 'ideas': with creating, choosing between, retaining, transforming, ordering, transcribing and developing their ideas. The research also highlighted the anxiety children experienced as a result of what teachers had come to see as accepted and unquestioned practices in school – for example, 'silent reading' time. Moreover, the study reaffirmed a worrying discrepancy that is known to exist between children's attitudes to literacy at home and at school (see, for example, APU 1981; Davies and Brember 1993). Why was it that children who were confident readers (for information) at home were reluctant readers in school? And why did children who claimed they chose to write stories at home find story writing in school such a stressful and unfulfilling experience?

In fact, the children were openly critical of several aspects of their teachers' practice. For example, the children spoke negatively about the use of planning sheets and the nature of the support they received when writing stories. In addition they criticised their teachers' right to choose – and choice of – story titles. But what appeared to be underlying children's comments here initially seemed like a contradiction: the children wanted more structure and support and yet, at the same time, they also wanted greater autonomy. Yet this apparent contradiction might help to explain the discrepancy between the children's attitudes towards writing at home and at school. It seemed that the children did recognise the importance of becoming competent writers; indeed, they indicated that they would appreciate more focused and direct teaching in this respect. But, it appeared, competence in literacy was important only insofar as it enabled the children to meet their need to interpret, explore and express those ideas, events and experiences that were real and of significance to them. For children, it appeared that becoming a competent writer was a means to a specific end: an 'end' that, they felt, they were currently being denied in school.

Thus if we return to the question, 'What can children tell us about the teaching and learning of literacy?' the answer would be 'a great deal'. Yet how often have the voices of children been overlooked? In this study some of the children's responses were unsurprising and confirmed what the teachers maintained they already knew; others provoked extreme concern. In many cases the children's comments encouraged teachers to revisit and question their current practice. For example, should the children be allowed – or encouraged – to read magazines and comics in school? How effective is 'silent reading' in developing children's literacy skills? How appropriate are 'planning sheets' for narrative writing? Significantly, through raising teachers' awareness of the complexity of the teaching and learning of literacy, this phase of the project supported teachers in their planning of a number of further investigations. It is these investigations that are discussed in Chapter 7.

It is important, however, to end this chapter with a note of caution. I commented above that while Year 5 and 6 children complained about a particularly demanding teacher, they also spoke with great pride about their achievements in this teacher's lessons. Children's voices are an important source of evidence that we can use to evaluate and improve our teaching. But it is only one of a number of sources we can use. Ultimately, we need to bear in mind that there is a crucial distinction between giving children what they want and what we think they need.

7   So where do we go from here?

The teachers maintained that involvement in the initial phases of the study had been extremely useful and had provided them with many new insights into the boys and literacy issue. But they also recognised the need to take action – to begin to implement and 'test out' a range of approaches. At this point, the question I was most frequently asked was: 'So where do we go from here?' While I was happy to talk to teachers about their ideas and to help provide some structure to their explorations, I also recognised that there was a need for me to take a step back and enable teachers to take greater ownership of the research. This chapter, then, tells the teachers' stories: what happened when they individually and collectively devised and 'piloted' a number of strategies that were intended to address boys' and girls' difficulties and concerns.

Reception and Year 1: Jacqui, Melanie and Gaynor

Jacqui, Melanie, Gaynor, as teachers of the three youngest classes – Reception, Reception/Year 1 and Year 1 – formed an action-research team. These teachers' explorations aimed to improve children's attitudes towards, and parental involvement in, reading. They were aware from an earlier phase of the research that reluctant readers – many of whom were boys – enjoyed reading comics and magazines. In addition, it was noted that parental involvement in children's reading was limited – even with the younger children. The teachers therefore devised and piloted three strategies which attempted to improve this situation: extending the reading material offered in school, encouraging parental involvement in the classroom and the use of 'reading buddies'.

Comics in school?

The teachers commented at the outset that parents might have concerns about their children reading comics and magazines in school. They therefore sent out letters to parents of the Reception and Year 1 children, explaining exactly what they were doing and why, and asking them to bring into school any comics or magazines the children had finished reading. The response to this request, however, was extremely poor. The teachers maintained that there were a number of reasons why this might have been the case. For example, it might be that parents considered these comics to be too expensive to give away, or were concerned that they were not in good condition. The teachers suspected, however, that the most likely reason for the poor response was that comics were not seen by parents as 'proper' school reading material – as Jacqui commented, 'I just felt that parents thought … this isn't valid.' The teachers maintained that they could understand this, and Melanie expressed her own reservations: 'I don't like reading them to anyone … got to be honest, I'll pick and choose the bits I like and … look at the rest. I've never sat and read a comic with my class … '

Parents in the classroom

A second strategy piloted was the direct involvement of parents in the classroom. The teachers maintained that they had always encouraged parents to come and help in the classroom although on this occasion a more formal invitation was sent out to ask for help with children's reading. There had been a 'reasonable response' to this request and the teachers commented that the parents' help was proving invaluable. Not only were the children enjoying reading to other adults and benefiting from this experience but also the teachers felt that the parents were gaining some insight into how best to support their children. As Gaynor commented:

> Some of the books have funny titles, funny names in there … I get comments back, 'She couldn't read the names', and I've said, 'Don't worry, not a problem, but did she get the *meaning* from the story?' And I try and get the parents to read the story to the children, especially if it's an unusual one … If they read it to them then the children are more inclined to want to read it back and it's not unfamiliar when they come across a word …

Reading buddies

A third strategy piloted by these teachers was that of 'reading buddies'. This activity was the result of whole-school collaboration, with children in the top Key Stage 2 classes being teamed up with children in the Reception/Year 1 classes. The older children visited the younger children once a week for 15–20 minutes. Gaynor explained: 'The older one prepares a book, the younger one prepares a book and they do a swap-over … read to each other … and then they choose a book ready for the next week.' Gaynor added that the 'buddies' were also asked to keep a record of the books they read and to comment on how well they felt they read them.

It was this aspect of the research that teachers felt had been most successful. They maintained that there had been a 'definite improvement' in these children's reading skills, although what was even more noticeable was the improvement in their attitude towards reading.

Jacqui's research

In addition to collaborating with her colleagues, Jacqui also undertook some explorations of her own. Of the three early years teachers, Jacqui appeared to be most convinced of the impact of gender on young children's approaches to literacy. She therefore began to make more formal observations of children working at the 'writing table'.[1] She explained:

> I have an observation sheet for the writing table where I jot down if I observe a child there ... I just keep a general look at the various areas throughout the day ... I jot down, for example, if a child hasn't been to the writing table previously, or if there is a new stimulus and what it is ... and what the children are actually writing or recording. *Are* they recording or are they just drawing pictures?

In addition, in order to encourage parental involvement in children's literacy development, Jacqui began making story sacks: brightly coloured bags which include a picture book and accompanying games and activities, as well as guidance for parents on how the material might be used. Jacqui explained that, in her view, the story sacks took away the pressure of a decoding and that the focus was on learning *through* the activities.

Jacqui wanted to discover how the children were responding to the story sacks. She therefore decided to ask parents for their comments – a strategy which, she maintained, also meant that the parents would recognise that their opinions were valued. She explained:

> I say it's for you to tell me what went well and what didn't go well and how you felt. I want parents to tell me ... the children enjoyed them, yes, but *how* did they work with them, did they find them too difficult? Was there something I could perhaps have put in? Was your child's attitude different when working with the story sack? So it's asking the parents to be proactive in adapting the story sacks and involving themselves.

Jacqui was also convinced of the value of gaining evidence from the children themselves. She therefore intended, at a later stage, to re-visit the issue of home reading with the children and attempt to ascertain how far and in what ways they felt the story sacks had impacted on their attitudes towards and attainment in reading.

As part of her investigations, Jacqui also visited a teacher in another school. Jacqui was aware that this school had a different, less 'interventionist' approach to the teaching of literacy, and she wanted to find out more about this. Jacqui explained that, in her class, while she valued children's emergent writing she also undertook more direct teaching, particularly in terms of letter-formation. The visit, however, did lead Jacqui to question her practice:

> Do you think that perhaps we're doing it too early ... you know, are we hot-housing? I really don't know. But ... they go to the writing table, they write with me and it's small, it's well formed and they show me and they're so proud of it. And it does work ...

School-based research

The teachers, and Jacqui in particular, had collected an enormous amount of data but maintained that it was difficult to find time to analyse this in detail. Jacqui also commented on several occasions that she worried about the validity of her explorations.

Despite these concerns, the teachers were confident that simply becoming involved in school-based research had had a big impact on their practice. Jacqui commented:

> It did for me because ... part of my observations have been on the writing table. What are children actually doing there? Are they just drawing pictures? So yes, it certainly has had a knock-on effect because I'm observing more of what is going on, because sometimes on a busy day, some of the children bring you things to look at and ... you're looking at them with half an eye, I certainly am sometimes. Now I will go over and I'll look at what they're doing and I'll ask them about it, and make more of an effort ... So, yes, it certainly has made a difference.

Year 2: Emma's research

In the early phases of the project the main focus of teachers' discussions had been on children's difficulties with writing stories and this was the issue Emma wanted to explore in more detail. Emma explained that she was concerned that, given the complexities of story writing, she was expecting too much from the children in her class and that this might have a negative effect on their attitudes towards literacy and learning. As a result Emma decided to change her whole approach to narrative writing. She explained:

> So this term the children haven't written any stories on their own ... but I'm doing oral work on ... the skills they require to write a story.

So we've been doing whole-class stories ... with me acting as the scribe. And we discuss beginnings, middle, endings and looking at how we can make stories a little more interesting. So writing stories is not as frightening a thing as before.

Emma maintained that she had found that this approach had been useful in a number of ways. First, she felt it was a more effective way of approaching story writing as she was involved in directly teaching key skills and processes. Second, while the children contributed their ideas, and therefore felt ownership of the story, she was able to provide on-going support and guidance on how the story might be improved. Emma commented that the children were 'amazed' and 'proud' of the end result. A further benefit was that the children were relieved of the pressures of transcription. This meant that they concentrated for longer periods and, Emma hoped, were also developing positive attitudes towards story writing in particular and literacy in general. In addition, through adopting this approach Emma had become aware that while the 'usual bright boys' tried to dominate these whole-class sessions, she now realised that there were a number of girls who also had 'good' ideas. Finally, by putting herself in the position of a writer, Emma maintained that she had gained some valuable insights into the children's difficulties – for example, she admitted that she also found it difficult on occasions to think of an appropriate end to the story.

But despite these benefits, Emma did have some concerns about this approach. Given that the teachers had talked about story writing being so central a part of primary practice – particularly in the early years – this was unsurprising. Emma admitted that she had asked the children for their views: did they miss having the opportunity to write stories for themselves? The answer was a clear 'no!'

As she gained confidence in this strategy, Emma was eager to find ways of maximising the impact of her direct teaching. She voiced her concerns that in a class of forty there were inevitably some children who were getting 'lost'. Emma maintained that in the future she intended to continue to refine this approach through working with smaller groups of children.

School-based research

Like Jacqui, Emma also had concerns about the validity of her research method. She admitted that she had not collected any baseline data, nor, other than the whole-class stories that had been written, any 'concrete' evidence of the children's work. Emma maintained that, given the other demands of teaching, while she might be listening and observing with a much more critical eye, she simply didn't have the time to make observational notes or records. She did intend, however, to talk to the children at the end of the year and to find out whether their attitudes towards story writing had changed; whether they had become more positive.

Emma was also concerned that these new ways of working would not be effective unless they formed the basis of a whole-school approach. She stated: 'What we need now is time to actually work out what is going to be the policy on this and how are we going to do story writing from the beginning to the end ... '

Years 2, 3 and 4 – Emma, Glenda, Paula and Gareth

In addition to her individual exploration, Emma collaborated with Paula and Glenda, the Year 3/4 and Year 4 teachers, and with Gareth who was responsible for working with children with special educational needs. These teachers had introduced a particular system of organisation for language activities: children worked in their 'base groups'. Glenda explained that the children were allocated to a particular group on the basis of reading scores, SATs scores, as well as 'a general feel of the children's maturity'. On four days a week, after morning break, the children worked in their English 'swaps' groups, as they were known. The teachers planned this work carefully so that the children from each class followed the same programme of activities but at different levels. In addition, every day in the week had a particular focus: that is, Tuesday was word-level work, Wednesday was reading comprehension skills, Thursday was sentence-level work and on Friday the children focused on some aspect of 'creative writing'.

Reading comprehension

These teachers chose to focus their explorations on reading comprehension. This emerged, in part, from the perceived differences between boys' oral and written ability; as we have seen, teachers referred to boys' interesting ideas in whole-class discussions, and the problems they faced when asked to 'translate' these ideas into written stories. Glenda maintained that teachers had an idea that, in comprehension tasks, boys were better than girls at answering questions orally, but that when it came to responding in writing they tended to give a quicker, shorter answer. They were curious to find out if this was the case and whether the content of a text impacted on boys' responses. Would it make a difference, for example, if the reading comprehension was based on a 'boy-friendly' non-fiction text?

A further reason for focusing their explorations on reading comprehension was that this was an area with which the children had difficulty in the Key Stage 2 English SAT. The teachers commented that changes in the SAT meant that all children now had to undertake a reading comprehension; preparation for the SAT had helped to uncover children's difficulties in this respect. Emma explained:

It's not until this that I've noticed that a lot of them come unstuck, whereas when you were just doing your reading, choosing a book and reading ... it's whether they can read. Yes, you question them about what they've read but it's not until last year that I thought ... Hang on, maybe I haven't given this enough time.

To begin their explorations, the children in each base group were given two reading comprehension activities over a period of three weeks. Glenda explained:

One was a fiction, story-type piece of text and the other was a non-fiction text and we planned the questions carefully so that, although we differentiated, each base group had the same *types* of questions. So they had two literal questions, one about language, one about meaning, one about prediction and so on.

The teachers acknowledged that they had not had the chance to analyse the children's written work 'in any great detail'. Time was (again) cited as a factor, although the teachers also indicated that they had been 'overwhelmed' by the amount of data collected. That said, the teachers maintained that they had marked this work with a much more 'focused eye' and that this had revealed that the children's responses appeared to relate more to their ability in written English than either to their gender or the type of text used. Glenda commented that this had been rather surprising. Having especially chosen content that they believed to be 'boy-friendly' (particularly the non-fiction text) they assumed that the boys would have done better. She commented: 'In fact when we actually looked at the work, I think if you took their names out ... on the comprehension ... I think you'd have trouble knowing if it was a boy or a girl.'

Teachers also noted that the ability to extract meaning from the text did not appear – as they had thought – to be directly related to children's attainment in 'reading'. Emma commented that some of the fluent readers had apparently 'not taken anything in' while two of her 'strugglers' had scored well because they had been looking carefully at the text.

Oral comprehension

A third activity the teachers devised was an oral comprehension. For this activity teachers identified a sample of six children in each base group – a boy and a girl of 'top', 'middle' and 'lower' ability in English – and an oral comprehension was administered to each of these children. I noted above that, in the initial interviews, the teachers indicated that in whole-class discussions the boys' comments and answers tended to be longer, more complex and more imaginative than those given by the girls. A decision was made, therefore, to tape the children's responses so that teachers could evaluate how far this was the case when undertaking a comprehension task.

The teachers commented that they again chose this text – a poem – carefully; they maintained that they had now become very conscious of the gender bias of any materials used in their teaching. But, the teachers noted, the actual process of choosing a poem also proved informative! Glenda explained:

> We were searching through poetry books ... it was Gareth, Paula and myself and Gareth said, 'Oh, I've found one' and Paula said at an identical time, 'Oh I've found one'. And when we looked at them Paula's poem was about when I grow up and a new baby in the family and Gareth's was on ... football – boys playing football and smashing a window... We decided to use Gareth's! [Laughter.]

Having listened to the tape, however, the teachers expressed their surprise that there appeared to be little difference between the oral responses of the boys and the girls. Moreover, when compared with the previous tasks, there was little difference between the quality and accuracy of the boys' oral and written responses. The teachers were puzzled by the apparent anomaly of their findings: why in relation to reading comprehension did there appear to be so little difference between boys and girls in terms of the quality of their responses? Why was it that boys appeared so confident when talking about their own ideas for a story (even if they found difficulty with writing stories) yet were so reluctant to voice their ideas and opinions relating to the text? As a group we considered various possible explanations.

One explanation related to the research method. The oral comprehension had been administered by a student teacher and, listening to the tape, the teachers realised that this had been carried out in what they perceived to be an inappropriately formal manner: as Emma commented, 'rather like a police interview'. This, teachers maintained, was hardly likely to have put the children at their ease. They also wondered whether the poem they had chosen for this task had been as appealing to boys as they had first thought. It was, after all, a poem; however humorous, it was very different from the kind of texts found in comics and magazines.

A further possibility related to the difference between the skills, effort and risk involved in expressing your own ideas and finding an accurate or appropriate answer in the text. Emma wondered, for example:

> With the comprehension, maybe girls are more confident because the answer's there, it's what the teacher's just read, it's not an idea that's going to be laughed at ... whereas with their own ideas they're not so confident ... Perhaps the boys are more confident with their own ideas, they like them being heard ...

Reading comprehension and SATs

As part of this phase of the research the teachers also met with me to review the reading comprehension activity the children had undertaken as part of the English SAT. In relation to the previous tasks the teachers had considered how the style and content of a text might impact on boys' attitudes and attainment. This task led the teachers to consider a further factor: the structure and presentation of an activity. For example, would it make a difference if boys were asked to extract information from a diagram or from a list of instructions rather than from continuous prose? And if the focus of the assessment was on extracting meaning from the text, would boys be more successful if they were asked to tick the correct answer rather than having to write in sentences? And what impact might boys' attitudes or preferred learning style have on their attainment? For example, the teachers noted that some of the boys tended to give an obvious 'common-sense' answer to questions without reading the text – as Emma commented, 'I think some of them thought, I *know* about this … why read it!' Was this related to boys' confidence or idleness (or both)?

Ultimately, the teachers agreed that identifying children's problems with reading comprehension was much more complex than they had initially realised. They were unsure whether the difficulty lay with, for example: decoding; understanding what the question demanded; the ability to extract information and meaning from the text or to empathise with the characters; the ability to form and write extended sentences; the confidence to express their ideas and opinions; the willingness to persevere when faced with a lengthy, dense text or a text which did not immediately spark an interest … or something else entirely!

Changing practice

The teachers maintained that analysing the demands of a task in this way was not something that they had ever attempted before. Paula noted that in the past they had presumed that 'if children can read then they can do reading comprehension'. Glenda elaborated that:

> In the past, if the children had difficulties with this we might have said 'Comprehension work – we need to do more of it.' It was quantity not quality. Now we want to find out, where is it that they're falling down? So, can they read it, first of all? If they can read it, do they understand it? If they do understand it, can they turn it round so that they can reform it in their own words? And then do they understand what the questions are asking them? Because just doing Key Stage 1 SATs, they often can read it perfectly and then they can't do what's expected of them … I think they often don't know what a 'what' or a 'which' or a 'why' requires. And, we thought, are we expecting them to suddenly understand what reading comprehension is all about?

As the following discussion makes clear, what emerged strongly was the felt need for more direct instruction – more 'teaching' of skills.

PAULA: What we've come to say is that we need to actually teach the children specific skills and not just expect them to be able to read a passage and answer it. I don't think we've ever taught them ... how *do you* do a reading comprehension, we just presume that they know how to do it and they don't ... So what we want to try and do now is do more teacher-led work.

GARETH: Teach the skills – and see if there's an improvement.

PAULA: We listen to them read every week, you know, but we're not actually teaching them how to extract information from the reading and how to really make sense of what it means.

GLENDA: It really has had an impact on our planning in the sense that we realise now it's no good doing more comprehension work in class – it's probably better to do less of the way that we've been doing it and should go at it from a different angle ... . Yes, this is it, to get the children talking more about the questions that they find difficult. I think there's a reluctance to have an oral lesson where there's no written work done, but we feel we need to do far more of that next year and actually get the children's ideas drawn out ... If there's a particular question or type of question that they're finding particularly difficult, why is that? And maybe working towards solving it together.

PAULA: Because at the moment, I mean the way we've worked is, they do the reading comprehension, it's marked and that's it. It's never gone back and re-visited and, they're not helped, are they?

GLENDA: The other thing I think we're so, we're always trying to be so positive, we never actually say, 'No, you're wrong'. [Laughter.] 'You've done that wrong, you're completely on the wrong track' and we don't think we're going do that next year but we're going to say to them maybe you could have done this, or done that. Perhaps we ought to focus more on where they are going wrong ...

EMMA: ... be more explicit.

GARETH: More whole-class teaching, as well. Instead of just giving them work sheets and thinking, they can do it – think about preparation and also the follow-up and give it more time really. Because I think sometimes we think we've got to do this today and something else tomorrow and, you know, mark it right away – give it more time.

PAULA: Yeah, back to basics ...

However, these teachers also recognised that if they were to be effective in improving this area of children's literacy, there was a need to adopt a whole-school approach and to map out a progression of skills and how they should be taught in each year group.

School-based research

While the teachers were enthusiastic about their involvement in this research, like the early years teachers, they also had concerns about the research process. First, as indicated above, their initial explorations had resulted in a mass of data which they felt they did not have time to analyse in detail. As Paula maintained: 'Collecting data is a lot easier than analysing it!'

The teachers also voiced a concern that their investigations did not match up to the rigour of 'proper' research and recognised that in this project any evaluation of improvement would have to rely, at least in part, on their own professional judgement. Ultimately, the teachers maintained that they had begun to appreciate the importance of considering, in advance, what evidence it was prudent to collect in order to evaluate the children's progress – that is, baseline evidence. This, they maintained, was something they would consider when they began their more formal investigations in the following year as part of the LEA literacy project.

Top Key Stage 2: Simon, Amanda and Christine

Simon, Amanda and Christine, the three teachers who taught the top Key Stage 2 classes (Year 5, Year 5/6 and Year 6) also organised the children into 'base groups' for language work and collaborated in planning a programme of activities. These teachers chose to focus their exploration on two issues that had been highlighted in the interviews with the children (see Chapter 6): the use of planning sheets for story writing and 'silent reading'.

Planning sheets

The teachers recognised that many children appeared reluctant to plan their stories. Simon commented, for example that they 'just want to go ahead and get started without giving it much thought'. He maintained that, while some children did not see the relevance of making a plan, others appeared to struggle with the process of planning: they found it difficult to think up, identify or articulate key points or ideas. This led the teachers to discuss the demands of planning: did children have to be able to hold a mental map of the whole story before beginning to write? And was this the way children – or authors – wrote stories? Amanda commented that she had attended a number of workshops on developing children's writing and had been given conflicting advice on this point. She stated:

> We teach them to plan their stories, you have to think of a beginning, a middle and an end and this author said, 'Oh, you don't want to plan these stories, you just go ahead, go for it … ' And then others want to

talk about planning. I mean everybody obviously does it in different ways.

But while the teachers understood children's reluctance and difficulties, they also recognised that when they did not make a plan, the children often failed to complete their stories – particularly in the English SAT. The teachers were convinced of the need for some sort of framework that the children could bring to mind in an examination situation. As Christine commented: 'I can't think of anything more terrifying than a 10-year-old having 15 minutes to sit there with a blank sheet of paper. ... *I'd* find it absolutely awful.'

Simon, who worked with the 'lower ability' children, involved his class in devising a basic writing frame. Amanda and Christine collaborated on a new design for their classes. This incorporated similar headings to the previous planning sheet but, in order to help the children remember key ideas, was based on the mnemonic BIG IDEAS:

Beginnings: where, when and how does the story begin? Jot down ideas for an amazing, intriguing or gripping opening sentence. Get the reader's interest!

Ideas. Jot down your first excellent brain waves here as they come to you!

Go for bullet points. Plan as you go, before you start or a bit of both!

Inspirations! Don't let good ideas go to waste! Put them here to use later.

Description. Always a good ingredient for a super story. Take a break from all the action to let the reader know what it's really like to be in your story. Jot down words and phrases which really show what your characters and places are like.

Ending. You can plan this at any time. Don't let your story fizzle out! Keep the reader guessing until the end. How about a dramatic final sentence?

Action. For maximum impact present the action in a couple of short bursts in different parts of the story. Who or what is involved? Is there a build-up?

Speech. What kind of thing would your characters really say? Two or three bits of dialogue are plenty. What words can you use instead of 'said'?

Planning sheets and school-based research

Even at this early stage the teachers were curious to find out whether these frameworks had improved children's writing. The teachers recognised the need to gather data in order to monitor and evaluate progress and had collected samples of children's plans and stories. They also intended to use the Key Stage 2 English SAT as 'evidence'. However, these teachers, like their colleagues, worried about data analysis: not only would it demand a great deal of time but it was not something that they felt confident in attempting without 'outside' support.

A meeting was arranged with the teachers and, like the lower Key Stage 2 teachers, they chose to review the children's writing SAT. Having read and discussed the papers, the teachers expressed disappointment with the quality of some of the children's stories. They did note, however, that many of the children had attempted to organise their ideas under different headings; even though these did not always reflect the mnemonic that had been suggested!

At the end of this meeting the teachers were convinced that using a planning frame would at least have made the writing SAT a less stressful experience for the children. In addition, they felt that they had enough evidence to claim that the framework had impacted positively on the way in which many children's ideas were organised and structured and that it enabled the children – particularly the boys – to complete written tasks. But, they wondered, was this enough? Could they claim that the writing frames were effective and successful if, as yet, there was no marked improvement in the quality of the children's compositions – for example, in the effective use of description, action and speech? They decided that this was something they would need to revisit in the future.

Silent reading

The other issue under exploration by the top Key Stage 2 teachers was 'silent reading'. Like the use of planning sheets, this too had been highlighted in the interviews with the sample children. The teachers admitted, however, that they had been aware for some time that there were difficulties with this activity. Christine and Simon noted:

CHRISTINE: Well, it was unstructured and 'uninstructed' basically. It was called 'silent' reading but it was a joke, basically, because it wasn't silent in any way…

SIMON: And even if it was quiet, that was time for the teacher to collect bank money, raffle tickets and things like that and it really wasn't being used properly.

CHRISTINE: Yes, we felt we were just using the time to do things like that and to listen to readers as well but we weren't even getting through many readers in the time because of all the stopping to say, you know, 'Excuse me, can you be quiet', 'What are you doing?', 'Get a book out and …'

It appeared that it was the comments of the children (see Chapter 6) that had brought this issue into sharp focus and had also made the teachers aware that they shared common difficulties. Christine, for example, commented that:

… In the course of this research, the meetings that we had, people started to admit that silent reading just isn't that useful, whereas perhaps before they weren't quite so open about it. Nobody really said, did they? You just assumed it was just you, you know, you couldn't keep your class on task.

Questionnaire

In order to investigate this issue, one of the initial activities undertaken was to administer a questionnaire, asking the children their opinions about the silent reading period. The children were asked, for example:

- What do you do during reading time?
- Why do you think you have a quiet reading time every day?
- Do you like reading silently to yourself? Why/why not?
- Are your favourite things to read available in the classroom?
- What other reading material would you like to have in the classroom?
- What do you read at home?
- Do you read silently at home?
- Do you have any ideas about how we could make the best use of this time to make your reading skills better?

The teachers spent some time reading through the children's responses and these, they maintained, confirmed their worst suspicions! When asked what they did during 'silent reading', children had commented, for example: 'Chuck pencils', 'Chat a bit and read', 'Sometimes I talk to a friend quietly and sometimes I read my book and draw' and 'I look out the window.' Most children reported that they did not like the insistence on reading silently (even if this was not always upheld) and maintained that they would prefer to 'pair up and listen to each other read' or 'do more play reading'.

On the basis of the children's comments as well as their own observations, the teachers decided to make 'silent reading' time, in Christine's words: 'more group orientated with more pair work and more structure'. Amanda and Christine grouped the children according to perceived 'need': for example, one group were 'poor readers and poor spellers' and so 'needed to concentrate on basic skills' while another group were 'good readers but had difficulty expressing themselves clearly'. Amanda explained that, like Christine, each day she would focus her attention on a particular group and that each week the group moved on to another activity. Simon also operated a rotation system of activities although he allowed the children in his base-group to sit with their friends. The activities Simon devised for his class included: paired reading, using the reference library to research an area of interest, using reference books to create a quiz, using the Internet, reading and reviewing magazines for football programmes and graphic modelling.

What were seen as the advantages of this new approach? The teachers all maintained that they were now able to hear the children read more often. Christine commented:

> I just listen to them and ... it's just 'Read that little extract there from the magazine' ... or just read the list of words that they've found that day. And I find it more satisfying ... I feel as if I'm doing something and that there is more purpose.

In addition, this approach enabled the teachers to diagnose children's particular language difficulties. Christine maintained, for example:

> I've never noticed before that L had a problem with certain phonic blends. That was something I was able to identify ... just having spent 2 or 3 minutes working on an individual basis with her. I wouldn't have picked up on it in the same way if I was hearing them read a reading book.

Advantages were also noted in terms of the children's motivation and in the more positive and purposeful atmosphere; Simon, for example, maintained that there was now a much busier feel about the classroom and that the children came into school enthusiastic to get on with their tasks. The teachers speculated that the length of this session, that it was only approximately 20 minutes long, may also be a factor in this respect: the children, particularly the boys, didn't have time to lose concentration and get bored. The teachers maintained that the issue of the length of a teaching session was something they wanted to consider for the future, whether the children's work would improve if they organised activities into 'short bursts'. Overall, the teachers maintained that what was of particular significance was that 'We're now making reading time more of a *lesson*, rather than it being just a time when we read.'

Silent reading and school-based research

The teachers commented that while they were making a point of discussing progress and exchanging ideas they were concerned that they should also be collecting and evaluating some 'hard data'. Having initially used a questionnaire to ascertain children's attitudes towards silent reading they intended to administer a further questionnaire at the end of the term. As Christine wryly commented: 'At least they [the children] should be able to say something constructive now.'

But the teachers recognised that they were aiming to improve more than children's attitudes towards 'silent reading'. Rather, they wanted to improve their attitudes towards reading in general as well as their actual reading skills. How were they going to evaluate how far they had achieved this aim? Again, the problem of not having collected any baseline data was raised and these teachers (like their colleagues) maintained that they now recognised the importance of this in relation to future research. However, they also acknowledged that there was, in fact, a great deal of evidence that they collected in their day-to-day practice – such as children's on-going reading records. This, also, could be analysed in order to make judgements about the children's improvement.

Discussion and conclusions

In this phase of the project the teachers took control of the research: they planned, implemented and began to evaluate strategies which were intended to improve specific aspects of children's literacy. In some ways it was difficult for me to stand back at this point and observe – to support them from the sidelines. I was unsure about the direction of some of the teachers' explorations; I was concerned at the speed at which the teachers were appearing to move away from the 'boys and writing' issue and on to new aspects of children's literacy development. I later realised that this was a critical point in the project. It is only when teachers are 'doing it for themselves' that they can begin to experience both the demands and the delights of school-based research.

Undertaking their own research enabled some of the teachers to see the relationship between gender and literacy in more complex ways. For example, Glenda commented that she had initially assumed that as boys generally suggested 'good' ideas when discussing their stories, they would also give 'good' answers in both written and oral comprehension tasks. However, this proved not to be the case. The teachers speculated whether this finding challenged their initial perceptions or whether it could again be related to gender differences. They commented that the idea that girls are likely to be more successful in situations where there is a correct answer to be found while boys are dominant in situations where they are asked to voice their own opinions, did fit in with gender stereotypes. Moreover, if gender differences (stereotypes) were accurate, then it would be reasonable to predict that even those boys who were 'good' readers would be less willing to read the text carefully, having assumed that they already know the answer.

As well as challenging some of the teachers' initial perceptions, this research also led many teachers to confront their own values in relation to gender. I noted, for example, that when looking for a boy-friendly text for reading comprehension, Paula had chosen a poem about babies and families while Gareth had chosen a poem about football and smashing windows. It would appear that, even when considering boys' tastes, teachers' choices were related to their own gendered preferences.

The research also enabled teachers to see teaching and learning in more complex ways. Earlier investigations, particularly the interviews with the children, had made visible some areas of their practice which were problematic and, having become aware of them, the teachers were eager to address these difficulties. It was clear from the teachers' comments that close collaboration had been a significant factor in bringing about change: not only were teachers able to 'try out' and share their ideas, collaboration appeared to give them the confidence to experiment with new approaches and strategies. In addition, having discussed and agreed a plan of action, the teachers appeared to feel a sense of responsibility to their colleagues to carry this through.

The impact of this research on teachers' practice, then, appeared to be immense. In part, this seemed to be related to teachers' closer examination of children's difficulties. As we have seen, Glenda admitted that, in the past, if the children had experienced difficulties with reading comprehension the 'natural' response would have been, 'Let's do more of it.' This phase of the project had encouraged the teachers to ask questions about their practice: 'Why are the children having difficulties?' 'What is the precise nature of these difficulties?' 'How do they relate to the text or context in which the literacy task is undertaken?' 'What can I/we do to improve the situation?' In response to these questions the teachers maintained that they were now much more aware of the significance of structure in children's – particularly boys' – attainment in literacy. Moreover, having dissected the tasks and having become more confident about the nature of children's difficulties, they appeared more willing to engage in the direct teaching of what they defined as key skills.

One of the major concerns teachers had about their projects was the rigour and validity of their research. Undoubtedly this was a difficulty in many cases and I could understand teachers' fears that their research was not 'legitimate'. For some teachers (like the Key Stage 2 boys they had criticised) there had been an over-eagerness to 'get on with it' – to try out strategies – and a reluctance to plan, to consider in advance how they were going to monitor progress and evaluate improvement. However, for most of the teachers, this was a first attempt at school-based research and they viewed their explorations as a preparation for more formal investigation as part of a larger project run by the LEA. I also recognised that too great an insistence on rigour at this stage might have had a negative effect. Moreover, I reasoned that when teachers understood for themselves the need for collecting evidence this was more likely to become part of their research practice.

I attempted to reassure the teachers that while rigour was obviously something worth striving for, it did not mean that worthwhile gains could not be made by engaging in research that, in purist terms, was less than perfect. Undertaking school-based research is a skill – and like all skills can be developed and improved. In addition, I tried to demonstrate that evidence could be collected from a range of sources, many of which were part of (or could be adapted from) their day-to-day teaching routines –

such as observation, discussion with groups of children, samples of children's writing and reading records.

Finally, one factor discussed in previous chapters was the significance of what are seen as 'legitimate' literacy practices within school; this also featured in this phase of the research. For example, Melanie admitted that she had hesitations about using comics as reading material for children in school. In addition, when choosing a boy-friendly text for reading comprehension, it was noted that the teachers still opted for a poem rather than experimenting with text from, for example, a football or computer magazine. Only the teachers in the top classes appeared willing to make use of magazines in their restructured literacy activities. Why teachers might be reluctant to use such texts will be considered in Chapter 8 when I discuss the findings from the final interviews with the teachers and draw together some of the main themes emerging from this project.

Part III
Towards a resolution?

8 Looking back
Exploring the 'boys and literacy' issue

At the end of the school year I interviewed the teachers once again to find out what they felt they had learnt about the boys and literacy issue. Were the teachers any clearer, for example, about the nature and cause of boys' difficulties? A second area of interest was the impact of this project on teachers' practice. From our previous discussions I was aware that many teachers referred to radical changes in their approach to teaching certain aspects of literacy. I wanted to find out more about these changes and also to ascertain why they had taken place. Finally, I was interested in any impact the project might have had on teachers' thinking about gender and its relationship with schooling.

What, then did teachers feel they had learnt about 'boys and literacy'?

Boys and literacy

At the beginning of the project the teachers were clear about the numerous gender differences between boys and girls: for example, differences were noted in relation to attitudes, behaviour, use of language, transcription skills, and also reading and writing preferences. Moreover, the list of boys' difficulties with literacy was long: boys, the teachers maintained, were more likely than girls to have difficulties with spelling and handwriting. Their written stories often lacked detail and description and they tended to use the language of cartoons rather than the figurative or descriptive language the teachers wanted. In addition, while boys appeared more assertive than girls and often dominated classroom discussions, they were also seen as less attentive and more easily distracted, as needing more encouragement, harder to motivate and less likely to complete their work – especially longer and more challenging pieces of writing such as stories. Boys were also less worried than the girls were about pleasing the teacher or giving a wrong answer. On the other hand, when discussing their stories, boys were seen as having good ideas, and in general they were seen as being more creative and imaginative than girls were.

Having reviewed samples of the children's writing, the teachers modified their initial assessments slightly: they maintained that in relation to transcription (spelling, punctuation and handwriting), gender differences appeared to be less of a factor than 'general ability' with literacy. Children who had difficulties with transcription appeared to have the same difficulties no matter what form of writing was undertaken. However, these difficulties became more obvious when the task was particularly challenging. Moreover, in the case of a task which demanded sustained effort and concentration – like story writing – these difficulties became more and more apparent as the writing progressed (or declined!).

Following the study of children's perceptions, understandings about gender differences were modified further. From this study, it appeared that boys and girls faced many of the same difficulties with writing stories (particularly with 'ideas') and had similar reading preferences: they both enjoyed (or did not enjoy) reading non-fiction as well as fiction although by the end of Key Stage 2 their reading tended to be almost exclusively functional. Boys and girls were united in their views about good teaching, in their desire to write their own stories and in their dislike of 'silent reading' time and the use of planning sheets.

In the final phase of this research the lower Key Stage 2 teachers maintained that, in reading comprehension at least, there appeared to be little difference between boys' oral and written responses and between boys' and girls' responses – both oral and written. But, as I noted in Chapter 7, the fact that gender differences were less apparent in reading comprehension may, of course, have been the result of more complex interactions between gender and literacy. That is, boys' assertiveness and willingness to take risks may have positively impacted on them voicing their *own* ideas while their lack of concentration and perseverance may have had a negative impact when they were required to find an answer (someone else's answer) within a text. Girls, on the other hand, were more likely to feel secure knowing the correct answer was there to be found in the text but less confident when asked to volunteer their own ideas.

At the end of the project, then, it appeared that the only 'uncontested' aspect of gender difference related to children's attitudes, interests and behaviour, and how these influenced children's preferences in reading and writing and their attainment in literacy – in particular, their writing of stories. Certainly, from my own explorations of children's writing, it appeared that the content of boys' and girls' stories reflected – and were used to demonstrate – their gendered understandings of the different worlds in which they lived. It is interesting to note, then, that Ofsted (e.g. 1998, 1999, see Bunting 1999) suggest that compared with girls, boys have particular difficulties with, for example, handwriting, presentation, grammar and accuracy. Are the findings of this study, then, particular to this school? Or is there another explanation?

In earlier chapters, I noted that it is claimed that gender differences are most apparent at the extremes of the ability range (e.g. Gorard *et al.*

1999). In this study the teachers maintained that in relation to language work there appeared to be a broad pattern of ability distribution in each class: there tended to be some very good boys at the top, mainly girls in the middle band and a long tail of boys at the lower end. This meant, of course, that there tended to be more boys than girls in the 'lower ability' language groups. Had difficulties with writing – in particular, with transcription – became 'owned' by boys? As there were more boys who struggled with writing, had these difficulties become associated with their gender rather than simply being viewed as difficulties faced by all poor writers? And does this represent another shift in attitude that helps to explain the current media interest in biological determinism (Chapter 2)? That is, rather than (or as well as) being related to a lack of effort and interest, boys' difficulties with literacy are seen as both intrinsic to their genetic make-up and beyond their control.

In the final project interview, it was noted that the teachers appeared to find it difficult to articulate what they felt they had learned about the boys and literacy issue; instead, they commented on what they had *done*: the strategies they had implemented. It was noted, also, that rather than making generalised statements about boys and girls as they had done in the initial interview, the teachers tended to focus on the strengths and difficulties of individual children. Christine, for example, referred to one girl, T, who, she maintained, was more motivated than many of the boys and 'who was likely to write and write and write' (stereotypical girl). But, she added, 'then again, I think T's not really bothered about the quality of the work ... she just wants to get it finished, doesn't she?' (non-stereotypical girl). In part, such comments simply reflect the world of action in which these teachers lived, although they may also indicate that the boys and literacy issue was now seen in more complex ways. It is likely, as MacDonald *et al.* (1999) point out, that there is more variance to be found *within* groups of boys and groups of girls (which may be related to a range of other factors, including class, race and poverty) than *between* boys and girls as a whole.

But recognising the complexity of this issue had certain disadvantages. Glenda, for example, expressed her frustration (which appeared to be held by many of the teachers) that, despite all their thinking, reading, discussion, action and reflection, they *still* did not fully understand the nature of the problem. As Glenda commented:

> Although we've made some roads into it, I still don't think we've actually got to the bottom of the problem. So, although we've become much more aware of certain issues ... much more gender aware ... in selecting materials, selecting books ... I think our knowledge has increased but I still wonder whether we've got to the bottom of the problem or whether we've just chipped away at the edge of it.

The impact of the project

Despite this concern, the teachers all maintained that involvement in this project had radically changed their practice. As we saw in Chapter 7, one of the most significant of these changes was a greater emphasis on direct teaching and the use of structure. This approach included the use of various writing frames, breaking down longer pieces of language work into smaller sub-sections, as well as the focused teaching of specific literacy skills. As Amanda commented: 'My style of teaching is more structured, more focused, more purposeful, more together really.'

One of the areas in which this new approach was most visible was in the teaching of story writing. The complexity of writing has long been recognised by researchers working in this field. For young children, speech is the primary discourse and thus in learning to write they are having to learn to operate in a new (secondary) discourse with many different processes and demands (Bunting 1999). Cambourne (1988, 1995, cited in Smith and Elley 1998) maintains that writers have to undertake a number of largely subconscious decisions and draw on a 'linguistic data pool' of knowledge about forms of words and ways of sequencing them in order to make those decisions. Thus, according to Cambourne, when writing a story children not only have to consider topic, purpose and audience:

> he/she would call on the data pool for the general features of narrative (setting, characters, plot, complication, resolution, conclusion) and use such a framework – still unconsciously – to organise the writing. The data pool would also be called on to provide appropriate conventions, words, and categories of words – to allow suitable words for the setting (descriptive), words for events that happened (past tense verbs), dialogue (speech marks), language to entertain, and so on.
>
> (cited in Smith and Elley 1998: 62)

Having articulated (and in Emma's case experienced) the demands of writing stories – both the cognitive demands and, for some children, the physical demands as well – teachers gradually changed the way in which they taught story writing in school. By the end of the year, like Emma, the teachers no longer asked children to write their own stories but instead focused their teaching on particular aspects of the story writing process – for example, reading, analysing and discussing published stories, the direct teaching of punctuation and grammar, and shared writing focusing on, for example, story beginnings or endings.

What had been the impact of this strategy? The teachers maintained that it was too soon to evaluate its effectiveness accurately. Christine indicated that she did not think this would be a 'miracle solution' to children's difficulties with story writing but, if nothing else, it appeared to 'take the pressure off' the children. Moreover, the teachers were all convinced that both boys and girls demonstrated more positive attitudes towards, and attained a higher standard of writing in, tasks that were short, clearly defined and highly structured.

The problem with stories – SATs

By the end of the project, it was noted that some of the teachers were beginning to question why so much emphasis was placed on story writing in school. One 'external' factor which emerged as having a particular impact on teachers' practice in relation to story writing was the English SAT. The teachers commented that their role, in part at least, was to prepare children for the SAT: to ensure that every child had a fair chance of doing as well as they could do. Indeed, one of the main reasons teachers gave for specifying story titles and asking children to write within a particular time frame was that it was 'good practice for the SAT'. The teachers also commented that when the English SAT was introduced, it was clearly 'story-based' – particularly at Key Stage 1 – and so story writing had inevitably been a key focus of their literacy work. In recent years, however, the SAT had moved away from this narrow focus and consequently story writing was now seen as only one small part of the children's writing. These teachers indicated that while a focus on stories afforded those 'literacy-capable' children the opportunity to achieve high grades, less capable children were more likely to achieve at least the average or expected grades through opting for other forms of writing.

As well as changing their approach to the teaching of story writing, therefore, teachers began to make more and more use of non-fiction texts as well as planning activities which focused on writing for different purposes and in different genres. Christine, in particular, voiced her concerns about the usefulness of story writing. She stated:

> Since starting this project I've really changed my mind about that. I think there are so many other forms of writing that are … more useful and more relevant … like letter writing and discussion writing, argument writing, persuasive writing – I think they're developing more useful skills, to be honest. Useful to them as people, as adults. And relevant to them as well, because they can write something for a purpose, a real purpose, whereas a story is hardly ever for a purpose unless they're going to entertain somebody with it. So since I've thought about it as part of this project, I'm thinking well, why are we making them write stories all the time?

In addition, Simon commented that focusing their teaching on skills such as report writing ensured that the children developed tools which were useful across many different curriculum areas. Of course, a further (unintended) consequence of this change of approach was that boys' difficulties – so noticeable in story writing – were less visible when writing in other forms. In short, then, in moving away from story writing based on an initial stimulus towards more structured writing in different forms, teachers appeared to have shifted from a creative or process writing approach towards a genre-based approach to writing.

From creative writing to the genre approach

Lewis and Wray (1995) note that in the 1960s and 1970s, criticisms of the formal, sterile and grammar-based approach to teaching writing gave rise to the introduction of what they call the 'creative writing' movement. Lewis and Wray comment that this approach was characterised by the focus on encouraging a personal response to a stimulus 'which would unlock a piece of creative writing from the souls of our pupils!' (1995: 13). This approach, which essentially concentrated on narrative writing, was also criticised, not only for its narrowness of focus but also for its lack of purpose.

Lewis and Wray (1995) maintain that the narrowness of children's writing experiences in school was also highlighted by the work of James Britton. Britton (1972) categorised language into three rhetorical modes: the expressive, the poetic and the transactional; the transactional being the mode of 'getting things done'. This included, for example, attempting to persuade as well as giving instructions or advice. Moreover, like the *Bullock Report* (DES 1975), Britton and his colleagues also emphasised the importance of encouraging children to write for audiences outside the classroom.

In the 1980s, researchers such as Frank Smith (1982) and Donald Graves (1983) placed an emphasis on the process approach to writing. Those who advocated this approach maintained the importance of children having ownership of their writing and going through the same processes as any adult writer: generating ideas, drafting, revision, editing and publishing. In relation to their writing, it was advocated that children take on the roles of author (composition) and secretary (transcription). Both roles are seen as important although, as I noted in Chapter 5, Smith (1982) argues that young writers need to pay attention to the composition first and concentrate on the transcription at a later stage. As part of this approach, teachers support children during the process of writing (rather than simply marking the end product), and the children themselves are helped to reflect on their own development as writers (Bunting 1999).

This approach again emphasised the importance in children's writing of 'audience' and 'purpose', although this was linked, in particular, with non-narrative writing (Collins 1998). Lockwood (1996) comments on the importance of moving beyond the normal readership of children's writing (pupils and teachers) and beyond the usual purposes (to demonstrate competence in particular, knowledge, understanding or skills). While the main purpose of narrative writing is to entertain, non-narrative writing aims (also) to inform, persuade and instruct (Collins 1998).

Bunting (1999) notes that research and inspection reports undertaken from the time of the *Plowden Report* (CACE 1967) have raised concerns about the amount of story writing done in primary schools, and have advocated the need for more 'sustained, independent and extended writing' (Ofsted 1993: 8). As well as ensuring authentic audiences and purposes, therefore, there is a need to ensure a widening variety of forms (Lockwood 1996). So what are these other forms? Bunting (1999) maintains that genre theorists have identified a number of principle genres including recount, report, procedure, explanations, discussion, persuasion and narrative. Lewis and Wray (1995) identify six non-fiction genres: recount, report, procedural, explanation, persuasion and discussion. These forms are said to be 'socially recognised text types' (Bunting 1999: 13): they perform different functions in written discourse and society (Barrs 1991) and are therefore seen as more meaningful in the adult world. Lewis and Wray (1995) maintain that, given their social origins, texts have particular internal structures which, through use, become conventionalised and seen as 'natural'. It is these structures which some genre theorists (e.g. Kress and Knapp 1992) maintain should be explicitly taught.

Throwing out the baby?

In adopting a genre-based approach the teachers were undoubtedly reflecting current thinking about writing. What, then, might be the future of story writing in primary schools? Given that this form tends to be related to personal expression (and child-centred education?), has story writing become irrelevant in the functional (adult-centred) world of twenty-first century education? And if so, what might we be at risk of losing?

Stories are a useful, some would argue an 'essential' human tool (see, for example, Wells 1987; Whitehead 1997). Andrews and Fisher (1991), for example, comment that often things do not make sense to us unless we think of them in the form of a story: we use stories to explain things to ourselves and to predict how things might turn out. They state:

> Stories and other narratives are one of the ways we can remember and share common experience, and in this way act as a bond in our society – whether it be amongst the family, a group of friends or in the society as a whole.
>
> (Andrews and Fisher 1991: 6)

Dyson (1994) similarly comments that:

> Stories, whether told or written, dramatized or sung, are universal cultural tools for evaluating past experiences and for participating in the social present. Within and through stories, we fashion our relation-

ships with others, joining with them, separating from them, expressing in ways subtle and not our feelings about the world around us.

(Dyson 1994: 220)

Moreover, stories are often essentially concerned with moral questions about good and evil, weak and strong. But within our society these bipolar categories are also gendered: reading and writing stories provide a means through which children work out and demonstrate their developing understanding of what it means to be male or female. I suggested in Chapter 2 that there is the possibility that writing such stories might only serve to embed stereotypical notions of hegemonic masculinity and emphasised femininity. While we may not feel at ease with the nature of these gendered understandings, are we right to deny children this space to make sense of this important (primary) aspect of their sense of self?

Literacy and schooling

A further area of interest in this research was teachers' attitudes towards literacy – not only the significance of story writing in school but also the school's role in introducing children to particular types of texts. We saw in Chapter 7 that some teachers did not appear totally comfortable with using comics in the classroom and – contrary to the experiences of Millard and Marsh (2001) – this concern appeared to be strongly supported by parents. Moreover, when looking for a boy-friendly text for a reading comprehension activity, the teachers chose a poem rather than making use of, for example, text from a football or computer magazine. I noted that only the teachers of the top Key Stage 2 classes appeared willing to make use of magazines as part of their structured reading activities.

The reluctance to use such texts in the classroom is understandable. Marsh and Millard (2000) note how many teachers are reluctant to legitimise comics as classroom reading material on the grounds of bad taste: for example, images portrayed are often excessively violent (in the case of male characters) or over-sexualised (in the case of female characters). There is also a reluctance, they note, to use a genre where the visual image is so significant a part of communication. Visual images are often seen as being there to support beginning readers and, Marsh and Millard maintain, in the later stages of primary schooling children (as well as teachers and parents?) tend to 'measure reading ability by the density of print and length of texts that they can manage' (2000: 104).

What does this tell us about literacy in school? This project indicates that, for children, parents and many of the teachers, learning to read *per se* was not enough. What was also important was that children learnt that some texts were of more value than others. Moreover, in relation to the reading of comics and magazines, gender stereotypes did not seem to be the particular concern for these teachers. Rather, for many teachers there appeared to be a reluctance to condone texts that were not seen as 'legitimate' in the world of school; teachers, it seemed, were the gatekeepers of good literature. This was also true to an extent of writing: as we have seen, although many teachers admired the 'sparky', humorous language used by many of the boys, their aim was to encourage extended, descriptive prose. Does this, in part, account for the differences between children's attitudes towards reading and writing at home and in school? Marsh and Millard (2000) suggest that using children's popular culture can provide an important link between home and school and can be a means for introducing children 'to the recognised canon of texts' (2000: 186). That said, involvement in this project made me acutely aware that teachers are required to please a whole range of 'onlookers' – for example, parents, governors and inspectors. Opting to use such texts, therefore, might not be a decision they feel they are entitled to make.

Boy-friendly

The teachers speculated that the adoption of the genre-based approach, and teaching in a way that was more clearly defined and structured, could be seen as 'boy-friendly' strategies. The teachers stated that they were now much more aware of choosing materials and resources that would motivate boys: teachers joked that they were practising 'positive discrimination towards boys'. The teachers of the youngest and oldest children, in particular, maintained that they had been focusing on 'looking at their [the boys] interests and looking at the way that *they* learn best'. All the teachers felt that it was important to present more positive male role models in relation to literacy. They claimed that many of the boys still saw literacy as something 'a bit soft' and feminine. The teachers therefore intended to invite more male authors and poets into school to work with the children. At a time when the world of work (traditionally, the male sphere) is valuing female abilities and characteristics (Stainton Rogers and Stainton Rogers 2001) it may be that in primary schools (traditionally, the female sphere) the strategies teachers are adopting are becoming more masculinised!

Two points need emphasis here. In Chapter 1 I noted that some writers (e.g. Bleach 1998) have suggested that not all male teachers would offer boys a 'good' role model, and that some may actually exacerbate the problem of 'laddish' behaviour amongst under-achieving boys. After all, teachers do not live in a vacuum – they are also gendered beings. In the final project interview, for example, two of the three male teachers in this study maintained that they could 'identify' with the boys who immediately turned to the sports page of the newspaper. Simon, for example, commented:

> I must admit, when I was at school I fell into that classic band of not being interested in reading outside of school and doing a piece of work

purely to get it finished and really not too concerned about what was in it. I can relate to that situation ...

In addition, female teachers appeared to identify with girls: for example, Paula commented that, like the girls in her class, she could clearly remember that as a pupil her main aim was to please the teacher. It could be argued, therefore, that, given that primary teaching is a predominantly female occupation, girls are more likely to be disadvantaged than boys, given the commonly held view that for girls passivity is both normal and appropriate behaviour. Ultimately, we need to ask whether it is ethical to make judgements about the effectiveness of teachers solely on the grounds of whether they are male or female.

A second point relates to the types of texts used in schools. As we saw in Chapter 1, it has been suggested that tackling male under-achievement through emphasising boy-friendly books may be counterproductive, as it will only serve to entrench the macho attitudes which caused boys to fail in the first place (Ghouri 1999). As I commented in Chapter 2, the messages that books convey about males and females may be subtle but nonetheless pervasive. Moreover, it may again be girls who, in relation to the world outside school, are disadvantaged. The impact of this strategy in terms of girls' attitudes and attainment would need to be carefully monitored.

In fact, while all the teachers agreed that the use of structure and the direct teaching of specific skills was simply 'good practice' and would therefore benefit both boys and girls, the shift towards adopting other 'boy-friendly' strategies *did* concern some of the teachers. As we saw in Chapter 4, Emma and Glenda, in particular, voiced their concerns that a focus on boys' interests when choosing texts, and the adoption of teaching styles geared to boys' needs, might disadvantage some of the girls. Glenda again stated that she felt that it was 'unfair' if particular texts and strategies (such as an emphasis on competition and speed of response) were adopted *solely* on the grounds that they appealed to boys; teachers should try to meet the needs of *all* the children. Other teachers disagreed. Jacqui and Christine, for example, both felt that girls would 'cope' with the introduction of boy-friendly strategies, given that they were more adaptable than boys and had a less rigid gender-identity.

In the final project interview, a further area of interest was a consideration of what brought about the changes in teachers' practice: what strategies or approaches had been most effective?

Collaboration, reflection and the learning organisation

The teachers indicated that one of the most significant influences in changing their practice had been collaboration: this had given them greater insight into their own practice and that of their colleagues. The teachers admitted that they felt reassured to find that they were not the only ones facing particular difficulties, such as motivating reluctant writers and readers. Moreover, collaboration and, in particular, collaborative planning, had given them a heightened feeling of confidence. As Amanda maintained:

> I am far more confident than I used to be because I can fully justify it. I know that what I'm doing is based on the ideas of two other people as well ...

In more general terms, the teachers maintained that involvement in this project had led them to be more effective in questioning their practice. Paula explained that:

> You always question, but you do tend to ... keep going along the same track sometimes, you get stuck. Because you haven't got time to come out and look at it clearly again, you just keep going with the same thing ... The project's given me time to step back and think, 'Well, is this the best way of teaching certain things?' and reassess the way I do things.

It is recognised that collaboration between teachers and reflecting critically on practice are vital if the school is to succeed and flourish as a 'learning organisation' (Sammons *et al.* 1995; Stoll and Fink 1996). Learning organisations, as Stoll and Fink point out, are those in which 'continuous development and improvement are integral parts of their culture' (1996: 150). They are organisations that, for example, treat teachers as professionals, encourage teacher leadership and participation, promote collaboration and high quality staff development (Stoll and Fink 1996). The role of the head teachers would seem to be critical to the achievement of this aim. I therefore asked the teachers their views about the role adopted by Dave during this project.

The teachers confirmed that they were aware that Dave had been a significant factor in both steering the direction of the project and in its success. The teachers maintained that it was Dave who had 'planted' the initial seed of concern about boys' under-achievement. Moreover, he had been significant in 'driving the project on' through providing an overall structure as well as through his interest and enthusiasm. In practical terms, Dave had acted as a coordinator, arranging times for teachers to be interviewed, ensuring teachers had time to plan and discuss key issues and ensuring materials and resources were available. In addition, Dave had provided encouragement and support for teachers to attend relevant courses and conferences. Finally, the teachers maintained that they felt Dave had given them 'space' – he had given them room to pursue their own interests and draw their own conclusions. As a result of this, they claimed, they felt trusted and valued.

And what was the impact of my role in the project? As I noted in Chapter 3, the teachers also spoke positively about the significance of my role and commented that each of the research methods I had employed had been valuable to them as collaborators in this research. However, I had concerns about certain aspects of my involvement. In Chapter 7 I noted that teachers had experienced great difficulty with the analysis of the data and in this respect I feel my role could have been greatly improved. I commented earlier that the project did not have external funding. Given the constraints on my time, I had conducted the analysis of data 'behind closed doors' and had simply fed back the findings to the teachers for validation and discussion. This may have been cost-effective in terms of time, but it certainly did not support the teachers' development (their autonomy) as researchers, nor their sense of ownership of the data.

I noted in Chapter 3 that Mortimore (1998) maintains that within a school there are three broad phases to the process of change: initiation, implementation and institutionalization. At the time of the final interview the teachers were eager to make use of their findings to inform and develop a coordinated, whole-school approach to the teaching of literacy. Only time will tell how far a habit of school-based research has become embedded in the school's ongoing practice. From the evidence, however, it appeared that the school was well on its way to developing an identity as a 'learning organisation'.

'Zeitgeist'

As we have seen, there had been many changes in teachers' practice. The teachers made a direct link between these changes and their involvement in this project. However, I would be more tentative in making such a claim. It is certainly the case that, following the initial study, the teachers recognised that a problem they had attributed to boys' reluctance to be associated with anything seen as 'girlie' – the use of figurative or descriptive language – was not so apparent when they were asked to write poetry. Moreover, they realised that they approached the teaching of poetry in a much more focused and structured way. This, then, may have provided an initial stimulus for them to reconsider their views about gender and literacy, and the benefits of structure in teaching. Moreover, it might have heightened their awareness of the impact of structure when examining the writing of the sample children.

But many other events had taken place at the time of this project that were likely to have exerted an influence on the teachers. For example, even though it was not directly encouraged in Wales, the teachers were learning more about the National Literacy Strategy, and, with the support of the head teacher, they had been attending courses and conferences across the UK on recent approaches to literacy. Dave also encouraged staff to read and consider literature relating to the School Improvement and School

Effectiveness movements: indeed, he had written several articles on this topic. Moreover, as we have seen, their changes in approach – for example, the move towards direct teaching, the greater use of structure, the adoption of the genre approach to writing – is very much in the 'spirit of the time'.

Up to this point I have talked essentially about changes in teachers' thinking and practice in relation to literacy. A final area of interest was teachers' *attitudes* towards gender. Did they feel that their ideas about gender had changed?

Gender and schooling

While the teachers all agreed that they were now more 'gender aware', they also maintained that they recognised that this issue (like that of writing stories) was extremely complex and sensitive. In the final interview I asked the teachers whether they felt it would be appropriate to try and change boys' hegemonic perceptions of masculinity. The teachers were doubtful whether they *could* have a great impact on changing boys' thinking about gender, given that they were only one influence alongside many others – for example, parents, the media and peers. This, they maintained, was particularly the case for a school like their own which was in a 'solid working-class area' and where gender roles were often clearly differentiated and patrolled by fathers. Paula, for example, maintained:

> I think that would be very, very difficult in an area like this ... where the boys, the maleness of the boys here is so, I don't know, so strong from the fathers ...

Glenda similarly commented:

> On Parents' Night we often get comments, 'Well, he's a real boy', not just a boy, 'He's a *real* boy' ... If he's in trouble it's, 'Oh, he's just like his dad' ... Little bit of pride, there, you know, they *want* him to be like that, they don't want him to be like mum ...

And, the teachers maintained, it was not just the fathers who reinforced these attitudes but also the children themselves. Melanie stated that the children in her class appeared to 'feel uncomfortable' and 'made comments' about one boy who, when dressing up in the home corner, often chose to wear jewellery. Glenda also spoke of a Year 6 boy who had recently confided in her that: 'If you don't show everybody you're tough, you just get picked on.' These teachers maintained that, for the older boys in particular, the worst thing was being perceived as 'soft'. In this school and community, appearing tough was about survival.

The teachers agreed, however, that understandings about what it means to be male and female did impact on attitudes towards and attainment in school. The teachers maintained that if it *were* possible, challenging boys' commitment to hegemonic masculinity would be likely to benefit their attainment in literacy whilst also benefiting the girls, given that girls often appeared to feel dominated by boys in class discussions. But changing boys' perceptions was not enough. The teachers maintained that the girls needed to develop a different view of what it means to be female so that they would not allow themselves to be dominated and would be more 'adventurous' in their writing. In addition, the girls needed to develop a different view of what it means to be male. The teachers commented that the girls often reinforced 'macho' behaviour as being a desirable norm for boys through responding to less gender-typed attitudes and behaviour – subordinate masculinities (Connell 1995) – in a negative way.

However, as trying to change such attitudes and behaviour was seen as 'unrealistic', the teachers maintained that they preferred to address particular incidents of 'unacceptable' behaviour as they arose. Moreover, they argued that questions of values in relation to gender were beyond their remit as teachers. The teachers' discussions highlighted the complexity and sensitivity of this issue: did they want boys to be more like girls – to demonstrate stereotypically feminine qualities such as cooperation and compliance? Or did they want girls to become more like boys – to demonstrate stereotypically masculine qualities such as assertiveness and competitiveness? Or was the aim, instead, for both boys and girls not to be constrained to act in particular gender-typed ways? And, frankly, was it the role of the school to determine or attempt to intervene in this?

Ultimately, the teachers concluded that it was not: like the teachers in Figes's (1994) study, they saw their role essentially as preparing pupils for society 'as it was'. As teachers then, they felt that regardless of any broader, or far-reaching causes and consequences, in keeping with the School Effectiveness and School Improvement movements, their job was to raise pupils' attainment as it is defined by policymakers and, importantly, as it is measured by SATs. Given the pervasiveness of these movements, and given that autonomy is not a word easily associated with the teaching profession in recent years, this is hardly surprising. It is perhaps ironic that the introduction of the National Curriculum and assessment system, based on the principle of 'entitlement', may also have marked the beginning of the building of narrower and more rigid boundaries in relation to what are understood to be the aims and purposes of schooling.

Footnote: my reflections

Involvement in this project did not only impact on the teachers, it also had a profound effect on my thinking. Gender had been an area of interest for many years – as an infant school teacher in the 1980s I had responsibility for 'Equal Opportunities' within the school. Like the teachers in this study, however, this project made me more 'gender-aware'. I was disconcerted to find out that what I considered to be an essential and private part of who I am and the nature of my close relationships could be understood or explained in terms of myself as a gendered being. Moreover, by looking carefully at some of my reactions and responses, I came to recognise that there were occasions when my responses were driven by what appeared to be a deeply inscribed desire to gain approval: to be seen as a 'good girl'. As a result, the boundaries between myself as a unique and autonomous individual and the social world in which I live became less clear.

Above all, then, involvement in this project made me aware of the significance of power and resistance. Male and female stereotypes (such as the aggressive, assertive, competitive male and the caring, compliant, nurturing female) began to make a great deal more sense when viewed as characteristics that reflect and enable the maintenance of patriarchy. As Connell (1995) makes clear, in the 1990s we did not see the crumbling of the material and institutional structures of patriarchy so much as a questioning of the *legitimacy* of patriarchy. While, individually, males may no longer feel comfortable subscribing to hegemonic masculinity, many are content quietly to reap the benefits of the patriarchal system (Connell 1995). Moreover, it is likely that even females who reject the 'ideal' of emphasised femininity may recognise that, on occasion, given the system as it stands, it is to their advantage to use their gender to play the power game.

From this study, then, I recognised that for many males and females the opposite of power is not just powerlessness but also resistance. Within classrooms it appears that for males (as those that hold power in society), resistance to the dominance of female teachers is often blatant. For females, as the subordinate 'Other' (Paechter, 1998), resistance may be quieter and more subtle but equally tenacious. Perhaps, as I noted in Chapter 1, it is that over generations females have had to learn to be personally, socially and occupationally adaptable (Arnot *et al.* 1999) and are well practised at attempting to subvert male dominance. I commented in Chapter 2, for example, that, despite the attempts of an adult and male play-mate to position her in a supportive role, one young girl shifted the context of play into an arena (the home) where, as a female, she had relative power and control (Walkerdine 1989). Moreover, in this study, girls who found language activities difficult might also have resisted the writing experience. Girls' concern with presentation and neatness, for example, may have been an effective way of avoiding the more difficult task of finding ways in which to use language effectively. Similarly, girls may have found that 'keeping their heads down' was a useful strategy for keeping (negative) attention firmly focused on the more assertive boys.

The significance of power and resistance also led me to consider whether there was another way of reading this tale of changes in teachers' practice. In Chapter 1, I noted that many of the strategies that have been suggested to improve boys' attainment appear to have unhitched school from society; they do not acknowledge the complex relationship that exists between school achievement, gender, poverty, social class and race. I do have some sympathy for this approach (and thus the School Effectiveness and School Improvement movements). Unpacking the numerous, inter-related factors that contribute to boys' under-achievement in school may only serve to paralyse and demoralise teachers. And, as Mortimore (1998) notes, schools can and do make a difference – although it should be recognised that they are one of a number of influences on children's lives.

What I am suggesting, therefore, is that, as the complexities of the boys and literacy issue became more apparent, the teachers in this project rede-fined the nature of the problem. I noted above that, as the project progressed, rather than seeing boys' difficulties as being related to *gender*, they saw them as being related to *literacy*. As such, these difficulties became associated with teachers' practice – as Glenda commented, they became a problem of motivation and effective teaching. In so doing, the teachers both brought boys' difficulties within their sphere of influence while, at the same time, positioned themselves as in some way to blame for these difficulties. At the risk of resorting to stereotypes, as a female, this sounds all too familiar.

Notes

Introduction

1 'St Thomas' and the names of the teachers are not pseudonyms: both before and after reading the text the staff felt that it was appropriate that they should be identified.

1 The context: a problem of gender

1 Given the complex relationship between sex and gender, it is unsurprising that these terms are often used interchangeably – for example, some writers refer to 'sex-stereotyping' and others to 'gender-stereotyping'. In this book, for the sake of clarity and coherence, I use one term – gender – although this is not intended to imply that 'gender' is discrete from 'sex' or that it is necessarily purely social in origin.

2 Hegemony, a concept derived from the work of Antonio Gramsci, attempts to explain how a dominant group maintains control so successfully that its view is accepted as 'normal' or 'common sense' (Paechter 1998). Hegemonic masculinity is a cultural ideal of masculinity that supports the domination of males and the subordination of females (Connell 1995).

3 There is evidence (see Pickering 1997) that suggests that while females do perform slightly better than boys in coursework, it is the examination paper that contributes most to their overall result.

4 For a review of boys' and girls' cognitive styles see Head (1996).

5 It was reported (Petre 1998) that men (although obviously not women!) have traditionally been deterred from working in primary schools by low pay.

2 Gender differences and their impact on reading and writing

1 Kimura (1992), whilst upholding the idea of sex difference in the brain, has challenged this finding.

2 This exposure, it is claimed, also slows down the growth of the left hemisphere in males, allowing the right hemisphere to develop faster (Stainton Rogers and Stainton Rogers 2001).

3 It is interesting to note how this suggestion appears to be supported by statistical analysis from the SATs, cited in Chapter 1.

4 See Golumbok and Fivush (1994) and Beal (1994) for an extensive review of this research.

5 This appears to reflect the argument of Fausto-Sterling (1992).

6 Paechter (1998) defines a discourse as 'a way of speaking, writing or thinking which incorporates particular things as given, unchallengeable truths' (1998: 2).

4 Teachers' perceptions of boys, girls and the teaching of literacy: 'It's the way they tell them'

1 An earlier version of this chapter appeared as T. Maynard and K. Lowe (1999) 'Boys and Writing in the Primary School: Whose Problem Is It?', *Education 3–13*, 27(2): 4–9.
2 Although I refer to children's 'stories', I am aware that writers have categorised text-types in different ways: for example, 'chronological' and 'non-chronological' (e.g. Perara 1994), 'narrative' and 'non-narrative' (e.g. Collins 1998; Andrews and Fisher 1999), 'fiction' and 'non-fiction' (e.g. Lewis and Wray 1995) as well as 'fiction and poetry' and 'non-fiction' (DfEE 1998).

5 Taking a closer look

1 Riley and Reedy (2000) note that punctuation is often thought to straddle both categories, given that it is concomitant with the grammar and meaning of the text.

7 So where do we go from here?

1 For guidance on research methods see Hopkins (1993) and Bell (1999).

References

Alloway, N. and Gilbert, P. (1997) 'Boys and Literacy: Lessons from Australia', *Gender and Education*, 9(1): 49–58.

Andrews, R. and Fisher, A. (1991) *Modes of Writing: Narratives*, Cambridge: Cambridge University Press.

Appleyard, J.A. (1991) *Becoming a Reader: The Experience of Fiction from Childhood to Adulthood*, Cambridge: Cambridge University Press.

APU (Assessment of Performance Unit) (1981) *Language Performance in Schools, Primary Survey Report, No. 1*, London: HMSO.

Arnot, M., Gray, J., James, M. and Rudduck, J. (1998) *A Review of Recent Research on Gender and Educational Performance*, OFSTED Research Series, London: The Stationery Office.

Arnot, M., David, M. and Weiner, G. (1999) *Closing the Gender Gap: Postwar Education and Social Change*, London: Polity Press.

Askew, S. and Ross, C. (1988) *Boys Don't Cry: Boys and Sexism in Education*, Milton Keynes: Open University Press.

Barrs, M. (1987) 'Learning to Write', in *Language Matters*, vols 2 and 3, London: Centre for Language in Primary Education.

Barrs, M. (1991) *Language Matters: Thinking about Writing*, No. 1, London: Centre for Language in Primary Education.

Barrs, M. (1993) 'Introduction: Reading the Difference', in M. Barrs and S. Pigeon (eds) *Reading the Difference*, London: Centre for Language in Primary Education.

Beal, C. (1994) *Boys and Girls: The Development of Gender Roles*, New York: McGraw-Hill.

Bell, J. (1999) *Doing Your Research Project: A Guide for First-time Researchers in Education and Social Science*, 3rd edn, Buckingham: Open University Press.

Bem, S.L. (1989) 'Genital Knowledge and Gender Constancy in Preschool Children', *Child Development*, 60: 649–62.

Benjamin, S. (2001) 'Challenging Masculinities: Disability and Achievement in Testing Times', *Gender and Education*, 13(1): 39–55.

Bleach, K. (ed.) (1998) *Raising Boys' Achievement in Schools*, Stoke-on-Trent: Trentham Books.

Blunkett, D. (2000) cited in 'Test Results Show Lag in Boys' Literacy', *The Guardian*, 20 Sept.

Britton, J. (1972) *Language and Learning*, Harmondsworth: Penguin Books.

Browne, N. and Ross, C. (1991) 'Girls' Stuff, Boys' Stuff: Young Children Talking and Playing', in N. Browne (ed.) *Science and Technology in the Early Years*, Buckingham: Open University Press.

Budge, D. (1994) 'A World Made for Women', *The Times Educational Supplement*, 24 June.

Bunting, R. (1999) 'From Process to Genre: Recent Developments in the Teaching of Writing', in J. Graham and A. Kelly (eds) *Writing Under Control*, London: David Fulton Publishers (in association with the Roehampton Institute).

CACE (Central Advisory Council for England) (1967) *Children and their Primary Schools*, London: HMSO.

Cambourne, B. (1995) 'Toward an Educationally Relevant Theory of Literacy Learning: Twenty Years of Inquiry', *Reading Teacher*, 49(3): 182–90.

Cambourne, B. (1998) *The Whole Story: Natural Learning and the Acquisition of Literacy in the Classroom*, Gosford, NSW: Ashton Scholastic.

Carr, W. and Kemmis, S. (1986) *Becoming Critical: Knowing through Action Research*, Lewis: Falmer/Deakin University Press.

Cassidy, S. (1999) 'Gender Gap Widens to a Gulf', *The Times Educational Supplement*, 29 Jan.

Chodorow, N. (1978) *The Reproduction of Mothering: Psychoanalysis and the Sociology of Gender*, Berkeley: University of California.

Coffey, A. and Atkinson, P. (1996) *Making Sense of Qualitative Data*, London: Sage.

Cohen, M. (1998) 'A Habit of Healthy Idleness: Boys' Underachievement in Historical Perspective', in D. Epstein, J. Elwood, V. Hey and J. Maw (eds) *Failing Boys? Issues in Gender and Achievement*, Buckingham: Open University Press.

Cohen, S. (1987) *Folk Devils and Moral Panics: The Creation of the Mods and Rockers*, 2nd edn, Oxford: Blackwell.

Collins, F.M. (1998) 'Composition', in J. Graham and A. Kelly (eds) *Writing Under Control*, London: David Fulton Publishers (in association with the Roehampton Institute).

Connell, R.W. (1987) *Gender and Power*, Cambridge: Polity Press.

Connell, R.W. (1989) 'Cool Guys, Swots and Wimps: The Interplay of Masculinity and Education', *Oxford Review of Education*, 15(3): 291–303.

Connell, R.W. (1995) *Masculinities*, Cambridge: Polity Press.

Connell, R.W. (1996) 'Teaching the Boys: New Research on Masculinity, and Gender Strategies for Schools', *Teachers College Record*, 98(2): 206–35.

Crace, J. (2001) 'Girls 1, Boys 0', *The Guardian*, 30 Jan.

Dadds, M. (1995) *Passionate Enquiry and School Development*, London: Falmer Press.

David, M., Weiner, G. and Arnot, M. (2000) 'Gender Equality and Schooling, Education Policy-making and Feminist Research in England and Wales in the 1990s', in J. Salisbury and S. Riddell (eds) *Gender, Policy and Educational Change: Shifting Agendas in the UK and Europe*, London: Routledge.

Davies, B. (1989) *Frogs and Snails and Feminist Tales*, Sydney: Allen and Unwin.

Davies, B. (1993) *Shards of Glass*, Sydney: Allen and Unwin.

Davies, J. and Brember, I. (1993) 'Comics or Stories? Differences in the Reading Attitudes and Habits of Girls and Boys in Years 2, 4 and 6', *Gender and Education*, 5 (3) 305–20.

Davies, N. (2000) *The School Report: Why Britain's Schools are Failing*, London: Vintage.

DES (Department of Education and Science) (1975) *A Language for Life (The Bullock Report)*, London: HMSO.

Dey, L. (1993) *Qualitative Data Analysis: A User-friendly Guide for Social Scientists*, London: Routledge.

DfEE (Department for Education and Employment) (1998) *The National Literacy Strategy*, London: DfEE.

DfEE standards site: http://www.standards.dfee.gov.uk

Dyson, A.H. (1994) 'The Ninjas, the X-Men, and the Ladies: Playing with Power and Identity in an Urban Primary School', *Teachers College Record*, 96(2): 219–39.

Elliott, J. (1991) *Action Research for Educational Change*, Buckingham: Open University Press.

Ely, M., Anzul, M., Friedman, T., Garner, D. and Steinmetz, A. (1991) *Doing Qualitative Research: Circles within Circles*, London: Falmer Press.

Ely, M., Vinz, R., Downing, M. and Anzul, M. (1997) *On Qualitative Research: Living by Words*, London: Falmer Press.

Ember, C. (1973) 'Feminine Task Assignment and the Social Behaviour of Boys', *Ethos*, 1: 424–39.

EOC (Equal Opportunities Commission) (1992) *An Equal Start: Guidelines on Equal Treatment for the Under Eights*, Manchester: EOC.

Epstein, D. (1998) 'Real Boys Don't Work: "Underachievement", Masculinity and the Harassment of "Sissies"', in D. Epstein, J. Elwood, V. Hey and J. Maw (eds) *Failing Boys? Issues in Gender and Achievement*, Buckingham: Open University Press.

Epstein, D., Elwood, J., Hey, V. and Maw, J. (eds) (1998) *Failing Boys? Issues in Gender and Achievement*, Buckingham: Open University Press.

Ernst, S.B. (1995) 'Gender Issues in Books for Children and Young Adults', in S. Lehr (ed.) *Battling Dragons: Issues and Controversy in Children's Literature*, Portsmouth, NH: Heinemann.

Fausto-Sterling, A. (1992) *Myths of Gender: Biological Theories about Women and Men*, London: Basic Books.

Figes, K. (1994) *Because of Her Sex: The Myth of Equality for Women in Britain*, London: Pan Books (Macmillan).

Fontana, A. and Frey, J.H. (1994) 'Interviewing: The Art of Science', in N.K. Denzin and Y.S. Lincoln (eds) *Handbook of Qualitative Research*, London: Sage.

Fox, M. (1993) 'Men who Weep, Boys who Dance: The Gender Agenda between the Lines in Children's Literature', *Language Arts*, 70: 84–8.

Gaine, C. and George, R. (1999) *Gender, 'Race' and Class in Schooling: A New Introduction*, London: Falmer Press.

Ghouri, N. (1999) 'Football Approach Risks an Own Goal', *The Times Educational Supplement*, 4 June.

Gilbert, P. (1989) 'Personally (and Passively) Yours: Girls, Literacy and Education', *Oxford Review of Education*, 15(3): 257–65.

Gillborn, D. and Mirza, H.S. (2000) *Educational Inequality: Mapping Race, Class and Gender*, (Ofsted), London: HMSO.

Gilligan, C. (1987) 'Moral Orientation and Moral Development', in E. Feder Kittay and D.T. Meyers (eds) *Women and Moral Theory*, Totowa NJ: Rowman and Littlefield.

Gipps, C. and Murphy, P. (1994) *A Fair Test? Assessment, Achievement and Equity*, Buckingham: Open University Press.

Gitlin, A., Siegel, M. and Boru, K. (1993) 'The Politics of Method: From Leftist Ethnography to Educative Research', in M. Hammersley (ed.) *Educational Research: Current Issues*, London: Paul Chapman in association with the Open University.

Golombuk, S. and Fivush, R. (1994) *Gender Development*, Cambridge: Cambridge University Press.

Gorard, S., Salisbury, J., Rees, G. and Fitz, J. (1999) *The Comparative Performance of Boys and Girls at School in Wales*, Cardiff: ACCAC.

Graddol, D. and Swann, J. (1989) *Gender Voices*, Oxford: Blackwell.

Graves, D. (1983) *Writing: Teachers and Children at Work*, Portsmouth, NH: Heinemann.

Greig, A. and Taylor, J. (1999) *Doing Research with Children*, London: Sage.

Guba, E.G. and Lincoln, Y.S. (1994) 'Competing Paradigms in Qualitative Research', in N. Denzin and Y.S. Lincoln (eds) *Handbook of Qualitative Research*, London: Sage.

Hackett, G. (1999) 'Boys Close Reading Gap but Still Trail in Writing', *The Times Educational Supplement*, 8 Oct.

Hall, C. and Coles, M. (1997) 'Gendered Readings: Helping Boys Develop as Critical Readers', *Gender and Education*, 9(1): 61–8.

Hall, C. and Coles, M. (1999) *Children's Reading Choices*, London: Routledge.

Halpern, D.F. (1992) *Sex Differences in Cognitive Abilities*, 2nd edn, Hillsdale, NJ: Erlbaum.

Hammersley, M. and Atkinson, P. (1983) *Ethnography: Principles in Practice*, London: Routledge.

Head, J. (1996) 'Gender Identity and Cognitive Style', in P.F. Murphy and C.V. Gipps (eds) *Equity in the Classroom*, London: Falmer.

Hitchcock, G. and Hughes, D. (1995) *Research and the Teacher*, 2nd edn, London: Routledge.

Hopkins, D. (1993) *A Teacher's Guide to Classroom Research* , 2nd edn, Buckingham: Open University Press.

Jackson, D. (1998) 'Breaking out of the Binary Trap: Boys' Underachievement, Schooling and Gender Relations', in D. Epstein, J. Elwood, V. Hey and J. Maw (eds) *Failing Boys? Issues in Gender and Achievement*, Buckingham: Open University Press.

Jackson, P. (1998) 'What Is It Boys Can't Do?' *School Enquiry and Research Newsletter*, (Swansea LEA) Summer: 2–3.

Jett-Simpson, M. and Masland, S. (1993) 'Girls Are not Dodo Birds! Exploring Gender Equity Issues in the Language Arts Classroom', *Language Arts*, 70(Feb.): 104–8.

Jordan, E. (1995) 'Fighting Boys and Fantasy Play: The Construction of Masculinity in the Early Years of School', *Gender and Education*, 7(1): 68–95.

Joyce, B.R. (1991) 'The Doors to School Improvement', *Educational Leadership*, 48(8): 59–62.

Keats, D.M. (1997) 'Interviewing for Clinical Research', in J.P. Keeves (ed.) *Educational Research, Methodology and Measurement: An International Handbook*, 2nd edn, Oxford: Pergamon.

Kimura, D. (1992) 'Sex Differences in the Brain', *Scientific American*, Sept: 119–25.

Kohlberg, L. (1966) 'A Cognitive-developmental Analysis of Children's Sex-role Concepts and Attitudes', in E.E. Maccoby (ed.) *The Development of Sex Differences*, Stanford, CA: Stanford University Press.

Kress, G. and Knapp, P. (1992) 'Genre in a Social Theory of Language', *English in Education*, 26(2): 5–15.

Lakoff, R. (1975) *Language and Women's Place*, New York: Harper and Row.

Langlois, J.H. and Downs, A.C. (1980) 'Mothers, Fathers and Peers as Socialization Agents of Sex-typed Play Behaviours in Young Children', *Child Development*, 51: 1237–47.

Laycock, L. (1996) 'Narrative and Writing: Young Children's Dictated Stories', *Early Child Development and Care*, 116: 53–63.

Lepkowska, D. (1998) 'Minister Promises to Act on Boys' Failure', *The Times Educational Supplement*, 9 Jan.

Lewis, M. and Wray, D. (1995) *Developing Children's Non-Fiction Writing: Working with Writing Frames*, Leamington Spa: Scholastic.

Lightfoot, L, (1996) 'Lack of Role Models Holds Back Boys at School', *The Telegraph*, 18 Nov.

Lightfoot, L. (1998) 'Boys Are Left Behind by Modern Teaching', *The Telegraph*, 5 Jan.

Lloyd, B. and Duveen, G. (1992) *Gender Identities and Education: The Impact of Starting School*, New York: Harvester Wheatsheaf.

Lockwood, M. (1996) *Opportunities for English in the Primary School*, Stoke-on-Trent: Trentham Books.

Mac an Ghaill, M. (1994) *The Making of Men*, Milton Keynes: Open University Press.

Maccoby, E.E. and Jacklin, C.N. (1974) *The Psychology of Sex Differences*, Stanford, CA: Stanford University Press.

MacDonald, A., Saunders, L. and Benefield, P. (1999) *Boys' Achievement, Progress, Motivation and Participation: Issues Raised by the Recent Literature*, Slough: NFER.

McKernan, J. (1996) *Curriculum Action Research: A Handbook of Methods and Resources for the Reflective Practitioner*, 2nd edn, London: Kogan Page.

MacNaughton, G. (2000) *Rethinking Gender in Early Childhood Education*, London: Paul Chapman Publishing.

McNiff, J., Lomax, P. and Whitehead, J. (1996) *You and Your Action Research Project*, London: Routledge in association with Hyde publications.

Mahoney, P. (1998) 'Girls Will Be Girls and Boys Will Be First', in D. Epstein, J. Elwood, V. Hey and J. Maw, J. (eds) (1998) *Failing Boys? Issues in Gender and Achievement*, Buckingham: Open University Press.

Mallett, M. (1997) 'Gender and Genre: Reading and Writing Choices of Older Juniors', *Reading*, July.

Maltz, D. and Borker, R. (1982) 'A Cultural Approach to Male–Female Miscommunication', in J. Gumperez (ed.) *Language and Social Identity*, Cambridge: Cambridge University Press.

Marsh, J. (1998) 'Gender and Writing in the Infant School: Writing for a Gender-specific Audience', *English in Education*, 32(1): 10–18.

Marsh, J. (1999) 'Batman and Batwoman Go to School: Popular Culture in the Literacy Curriculum', *International Journal of Early Years Education*, 7(2): 117–31.

Marsh, J. (2000a) 'Teletubby Tales: Popular Culture in the Early Years Language and Literacy Curriculum', *Contemporary Issues in Early Childhood*, 1(2): 119–33.

Marsh, J. (2000b) ' "But I Want to Fly Too!" Girls and Superhero Play in the Infant Classroom', *Gender and Education*, 12(2): 209–20.

Marsh, J. and Millard, E. (2000) *Literacy and Popular Culture: Using Children's Culture in the Classroom*, London: Paul Chapman Publishing.

Martin, C.L. and Little, J.K. (1990) 'The Relation of Gender Understanding to Children's Sex-typed Preferences and Gender Stereotypes', *Child Development*, 61: 1427–39.

Maynard, T. and Lowe, K. (1999) 'Boys and Writing in the Primary School: Whose Problem Is It?' *Education 3–13*, 27(2): 4–9.

Measor, L. (1985) 'Interviewing: A Strategy for Qualitative Research', in R.G. Burgess (ed.) *Strategies of Educational Research: Qualitative Methods*, London: Falmer Press.

Measor, L. and Sikes, P. (1992) *Gender and Schools*, London: Cassell.

Miles, M.B. and Huberman, A.M. (1994) *Qualitative Data Analysis: An Expanded Sourcebook*, 2nd edn, London: Sage.

Millard, E. (1994) *Developing Readers in the Middle Years*, Buckingham: Open University Press.

Millard, E. (1997) *Differently Literate: Boys, Girls and the Schooling of Literacy*, London: Falmer Press.

Millard, E. and Marsh, J. (2001) 'Sending Minnie the Minx Home: Comics and Reading Choices', *Cambridge Journal of Education*, 31(1): 25–38.

Miller, J. (1996) *School for Women*, London: Virago.

Minns, H. (1991) *Language, Literacy and Gender*, London: Hodder and Stoughton.

Minns, H. (1993) 'Three Ten-year-old Boys and their Reading', in M. Barrs and S. Pidgeon (eds) *Reading the Difference*, London: Centre for Language in Primary Education.

Moir, A. and Jessel, D. (1998) *Brainsex: The Real Difference Between Men and Women*, London: Mandarin.

Moir, A. and Moir, B. (1999) *Why Men Don't Iron: The Science of Gender Studies*, London: HarperCollins.

Money, J. and Ehrhardt, A.A. (1972) *Man and Woman, Boy and Girl*, Baltimore, MD: Johns Hopkins University Press.

Morris, E. (1996) *Boys Will Be Boys? Closing the Gender Gap*, London: The Labour Party.

Mortimore, P. (1998) *The Road to Improvement: Reflections on School Effectiveness*, Lisse: Swets and Zeitlinger.

Murphy, P. and Elwood, J. (1998) 'Gendered Learning Outside and Inside School: Influences on Achievement', in D. Epstein, J. Elwood, V. Hey and J. Maw (eds) *Failing Boys? Issues in Gender and Achievement*, Buckingham: Open University Press.

National Assembly for Wales (1999a) *National Curriculum Assessment Results in Wales: Key Stage 1*, Cardiff: National Assembly for Wales.

National Assembly for Wales (1999b) *National Curriculum Assessment Results in Wales: Key Stage 2*, Cardiff: National Assembly for Wales.

NCC (National Curriculum Council) (1990) *What Are Writers Made of? Issues of Gender and Writing*, The National Writing Project, Walton-on-Thames: Thomas Nelson and Sons Ltd.

Nilan, P. (1995) 'Making up Men', *Gender and Education*, 7(2): 175–87.

Ochsner, M.B. (2000) 'Gendered Make-up', *Contemporary Issues in Early Childhood*, 1(2): 209–13.

Ofsted (1993) *The Implementation of the Curricular Requirements of the Education Reform Act: English Key Stages 1, 2, 3, 4; A Report of Her Majesty's Chief Inspector of Schools (1992–3)*, London: HMSO.

Ofsted (1999) *The Annual Report of Her Majesty's Chief Inspector of Schools (1997–8)*, London: HMSO.

Ofsted (2000) *The Annual Report of Her Majesty's Chief Inspector of Schools (1998–9)*, London: HMSO.

Ofsted (2001)*The Annual Report of Her Majesty's Chief Inspector of Schools (1999–2000)*, London: HMSO.

Oja, S.N. and Smulyan, L. (1989) *Collaborative Action Research: A Developmental Approach*, London: Falmer Press.

Osmot, P. (1987) 'Teaching Inquiry in the Classroom, Reading and Gender Set', *Language Arts*, 64(7): 758–61.

Osmot, P. and Davis, J. (1987) *Stop, Look and Listen: An Account of Girls' and Boys' Achievement in Reading and Mathematics in the Primary School*, London: ILEA.

Paechter, C. (1998) *Educating the Other: Gender, Power and Schooling*, London: Falmer Press,

Paley, V.G. (1984) *Boys and Girls: Superheroes in the Doll Corner*, Chicago and London: University of Chicago Press.

Pease, A. and Pease, B. (1998) *Why Men Don't Listen and Women Can't Read Maps*, Australia: Pease Training International.

Perara, K. (1994) *Children's Writing and Reading*, Oxford: Blackwell.

Petre, J. (1998) 'Labour Seeks More Male Teachers to Inspire Boys', *The Telegraph*, 4 Jan.

Phillips, A. (1993) *The Trouble with Boys: Parenting the Men of the Future*, London: Pandora.

Phillips, A. (2000) 'Clever Lad!' *The Guardian*, 29 Aug.

Pickering, J. (1997) *Raising Boys' Achievement*, Stafford: Network Educational Press.

Plummer, G. (1998) 'Forget Gender, Class Is Still the Real Divide', *The Times Educational Supplement*, 23 Jan.

Pyke, N. (1996) 'Boys Read Less than Girls', *The Times Educational Supplement*, 15 March.

Renold, E. (2000) ' "Coming out": Gender (Hetero)Sexuality and the Primary School', *Gender and Education*, 12(3): 309–26.

Riley, K. (1994) *Quality and Equality: Promoting Opportunities in School*, London: Cassell.

Riley, J. and Reedy, D. (2000) *Developing Writing for Different Purposes: Teaching about Genre in the Early Years*, London: Paul Chapman Publishing.

Rowbotham, S. (1999) *A Century of Women*, London: Penguin Books.

Sammons, P., Hillman, J. and Mortimore, P. (1995) *Key Characteristics of Effective Schools: A Review of School Effectiveness Research*, London: Ofsted.

Sarland, C. (1991) *Young People Reading: Culture and Response*, Buckingham: Open University Press.

Schofield, J.W. (1993) 'Increasing the Generalizability of Qualitative Research', in M. Hammersley (ed.) *Educational Research: Current Issues*, London: Paul Chapman (in association with the Open University Press).

Schulz, M. (1975) 'The Semantic Derogation of Women', in B. Thorne and N. Henley (eds) *Language and Sex: Difference and Dominance*, Rowley, MA: Newbury House, pp. 64–75.

Seidel, J. and Kelle, U. (1995) 'Different Functions of Coding in the Analysis of Textual Data', in U. Kelle (ed.) *Computer-aided Qualitative Data Analysis: Theory, Methods and Practice*, London: Sage.

Sheldon, A. (1990) 'Pickle Fights: Gendered Talk in Preschool Disputes', *Discourse Processes*, 13: 5–31.

Skelton, C. (1996) 'Learning to be "Tough": The Fostering of Maleness in One Primary School', *Gender and Education*, 8(2): 185–97.

Skelton, C. (1997) 'Primary Boys and Hegemonic Masculinities', *British Journal of Sociology of Education*, 18(3): 349–69.

Smith, F. (1982) *Writing and the Writer*, London: Heinemann.

Smith, J. and Elley, W. (1998) *How Children Learn to Write*, London: Paul Chapman Publishing.

Spender, D. (1985) *Man Made Language*, London: Pandora Press.

Stainton Rogers, W. and Stainton Rogers, R. (2001) *The Psychology of Gender and Sexuality*, Buckingham: Open University Press.

Stoll, L. and Fink, D. (1996) *Changing Our Schools: Linking School Effectiveness and School Improvement*, Buckingham: Open University Press.

Swain, J. (2000) ' "The Money's Good, the Fame's Good, the Girls are Good": The Role of Playground Football in the Construction of Young Boys' Masculinity in Junior School', *British Journal of Sociology of Education*, 21(1): 95–109.

Tannen, D. (1990) *You Just Don't Understand: Women and Men in Conversation*, New York: Morrow.

Thomas, P. (1997) 'Doom to the Red-eyed Nyungghns from the Planet Glarg: Boys as Writers of Narrative', *English in Education*, 31(3): 23–31.

Thorne, B. (1993) *Gender Play: Girls and Boys in School*, Buckingham: Open University Press.

Thornton, K. (1999) 'Boys Turn the Tide in Literacy', *The Times Educational Supplement*, 8 Oct.

Treneman, A. (1998) 'Will the Boys Who Can't Read Still End Up as the Men on Top?' *The Independent*, 5 Jan.

Walker, R. (1993) 'The Conduct of Educational Case Studies: Ethics Theory and Procedures', in M. Hammersley (ed.) *Controversies in Classroom Research*, 2nd edn, Buckingham: Open University Press.

Walkerdine, V. (1989) *Schoolgirl Fictions*, London: Verso.

Warrington, M. and Younger, M. (1997) 'Gender and Achievement: the Debate at GCSE', *Education Review*, 10(1): 21–7.

Warrington, M. and Younger, M. (2000) 'The Other Side of the Gender Gap', *Gender and Education*, 12(4): 493–508.

Watts, M. and Ebbutt, D. (1987) 'More than the Sum of the Parts: Research Methods in Group Interviewing', *British Educational Research Journal*, 13(1): 25–34.

Weiner, G. (1985) 'Equal Opportunities, Feminism and Girls' Education', in G. Weiner (ed.) *Just a Bunch of Girls?* Buckingham: Open University Press.

Weiner, G. (1994) *Feminisms in Education*, Buckingham: Open University Press.

Weiner, G. and Arnot, M. (1987) 'Teachers and Gender Politics', in M. Arnot and G. Weiner (eds) *Gender and the Politics of Schooling*, London: Hutchinson.

Wells, G. (1987) *The Meaning Makers: Children Learning Language and Using Language to Learn*, London: Hodder and Stoughton.

White, J. (1990) 'On Literacy and Gender', in R. Carter (ed.) *Knowledge about Language and the Curriculum*, London: Hodder and Stoughton.

White, J. (1996) 'Research in English and the Teaching of Girls', in P.F. Murphy and C.V. Gipps (eds) *Equity in the Classroom*, London: Falmer Press.

Whitehead, M. (1997) *Language and Literacy in the Early Years*, 2nd edn, London: Paul Chapman Publishing.

Witelson, S.F. (1976) 'Sex and the Single Hemisphere: Specialisation of the Right Hemisphere for Spatial Processing', *Science*, 193: 425–7.

Wolcott, H.F. (1990) *Writing Up Qualitative Research*, Newbury Park, CA: Sage.

Wolcott, H.F. (1994) 'On Seeking – and Rejecting – Validity in Qualitative Research', in *Transforming Qualitative Data: Description, Analysis and Interpretation*, Newbury Park, CA: Sage.

Woodward, W. (2000) 'Single-sex Lessons Plan to Counter Laddish Culture, Leader: The Trouble with Boys', *The Guardian*, 21 Aug.

Wragg, T. (1997) 'Oh Boy!', *The Times Educational Supplement*, 16 May.

Yates, L. (1997) 'Gender Equity and the Boys Debate: What Sort of Challenge Is It?' *Journal of Sociology of Education*, 18(3): 337–47.

Index